Trendy Bar & Nightclub Business Startup

How to Start, Run and Grow a Successful Bar & Tavern Business

By

Michael Sanders

Copyrighted Material

Copyright © 2018 – *Valley Of Joy Publishing Press*

All Rights Reserved.
No part of this publication may be reproduced, stored in a retrieval system or transmitted in any form or by any means, electronic, mechanical, photocopying, recording or otherwise without the proper written consent of the copyright holder, except brief quotations used in a review.

Published by:

Valley Of Joy Publishing Press

Cover & Interior designed

By

Julio Lopez

First Edition

Contents

Foreword 6

9Introduction.. 10

    Who Should Open a Bar? 12

What to Expect When Starting a Bar/Nightclub 16

    Profitability 19

    Restaurants by the Numbers 26

    30-20 Rule 27

Finding Money for your Startup 31

    Six Ways to Find Money for your Bar Business 34

    11 Documents You Need for Loan Application 39

    Estimated Cost of Opening a Bar in a Small to Mid-size City ... 42

    Estimated Monthly Expenses 43

    Estimated Monthly Income Calculation 44

Knowing the Market and Setting a Trend 44

    Limiting Your Theme Options by Elimination 46

    Naming Your Bar 49

    Other Considerations 51

    Brainstorm: Formulas for Trying New Creative Names 53

Putting Together a Business Plan 54

    5 Biggest Misconceptions about Business Plan 54

    Six Compelling Reasons You Need a Business Plan for Your Bar 57

    Market Research 63

    What Else Should be Included in Your Business Plan? 69

Legal Aspects of your Business 75

    Incorporating Your Business 76

- Legal Structure of Your Business 81
  - Sole Proprietor 81
  - Partnership 82
  - Corporation (Inc. or Ltd.) 82
  - S Corporation 83
  - Limited Liability Company (LLC) 84
- Applying for and Obtaining an EIN 85
- Opening a Commercial Bank Account 98
- City & County Licenses & Permits 98
- Additional Agencies to conform with 91
- Liquor License 93
  - Liquor License Checklist 97
- Insurance 99
- HOW to Find an Existing bar to Buy or Lease? 112
  - 5 Offline Ways to Find a Business for Sale 113
  - 5 Online Ways to Find a Business for Sale 114
- Finding a Suitable Location 119
  - SWOT Analysis 121
  - Seven most important factors to consider when leasing a facility 124
- Planning & Build-Out 131
- Signage & Menu 136
- Décor & Furniture 139
  - Sound and Lighting 142
    - Special Effects 145
- Supplies and Equipment 146
  - Buying or Leasing 149
- Management and Employees 151

- 10 step process on how to hire, train and retain employees. . 151
- Hiring 161
- Scheduling 164
- Online Employee Training Sites 166
- Finding Suppliers and Vendors 168
- How to Manage Inventory 172
  - Invoice 182
  - Sales Figures 182
  - Conducting the Actual Inventory 183
- Pricing, Profitability & POS..184
  - Understanding Penny Profit, Profit Margin, and Markup 188
  - Proper Gross Profit for a Bar Inventory 193
  - POS System 195
- Accounting & Bookkeeping 199
- Music and Royalties 202
- Maintenance and Cleaning..204
- Marketing and Promotion 207
- Proven Marketing Ideas 217
- How to Increase Liquor Sales 221
- Additional Revenue Ideas 226
- Keeping Things Fresh AND NEW 228
- Last Word 230

FOREWORD

For years I worked simply for the goal of making money, not because I enjoyed where I was. I gave up my dream to settle for a decent salary, but was unhappy and grew to resent the company where I was. Then, one day it just hit me: there are two types of people in the world; those who set out to make as much money as possible, even if it means doing something they hate, and those who choose to do what they love, no matter who much profit they earn.

The question is: why does it have to be either or? Why not both? My passion was owning my own Martini Bar, and after experiencing the corporate side of the business, I was ready to start my own adventure of entrepreneurship with my real passion for the bar business.

If you have a passion for something, then you will become an unstoppable force in that industry. Years ago, I made the most important decision of my life; to leave the corporate world and pursue my dream of owning a trendy bar that would create new interest in our city. By no means was it an easy process. I put in hours of hard work every day and still faced more failures and mistakes than I could count; the entire journey was an incredible learning experience.

But, after five years of stress, hard-learned lessons, and an infinite number of amazing positive moments, finally, I was able to own and operate two successful bars in the great city of Birmingham, Alabama.

As I was working on opening the 3rd and 4th location in Atlanta, I was presented with a very generous offer to sell all my businesses, an offer I could not refuse. So, I decided to sell my business and agreed not to compete for ten years in or around greater Birmingham and Atlanta area. But nowhere in that contract said I could not write a

"How To" book and teach people how to open a swanky joint in their own town.

I learned many valuable lessons from owning a business and wish that I had some sort of guide or instruction manual when I first started. That is why I decided to write this book; for other aspiring bar owners to use to help them overcome their fears and worries so that they can open a trendy bar just as successful as mine.

This book contains everything you need to know when starting your own bar business. From basic business practices to choosing the right theme and décor, you will learn the most crucial tactics and methods to successfully run a profitable bar and tavern business.

Here is an inescapable fact: approximately 70%-75% of all small businesses make it past the first year, and only half of all startups survive five years. Selling my own bars for a profit was not just luck, it was a lot of market research, branding, trial-and-error, and elbow grease.

No amount of dreaming or wishing could make my business a success; it was all up to me and how much effort I was willing to put into making it work. You too can be successful.

Your business can make you money and live the life of your dreams If you have enough passion for your bar to succeed and grow, it begins with one step in the right direction and taking action to make your dreams come true.

Before we start, I also wanted to say a big "Thank You" to Jennifer Holmes and Tim Hoffman, without their help this book would not have been possible at all.

INTRODUCTION

Have you seen how there are trendy new age Martini Bars opening up everywhere? Have you ever gone into one of these? Have you ever thought this might be a good business to be in? I am sure you know that bars are the only business that is truly recession proof. Even during the great depression, bars and taverns were the only business that was thriving.

First, here are some facts for you directly from statista.com, a reputable site that keeps various business-related statistical data.

According to Statista, sales in the drinking sector in the United States have steadily grown since the mid-1990's reaching 23.15B dollars in 2015. The sector includes bars, pubs, lounges, taverns, and nightclubs as well as other drinking places that primarily sell alcoholic beverages for immediate consumption.

The National Restaurant Association estimated that food and drink sales in U.S. bars and taverns would reach 19.9B dollars in 2016. This is a relatively small figure in comparison to the wider restaurant industry, for which food and drink sales were expected to rise to approximately 783B dollars during the same year.

As a smart and savvy business person, I am sure you can understand that we all want to be a part of an industry that shows growth and not loss. What better industry to be a part of than this? Especially when this sector has shown steady growth year after year for decades.

If you are not 100% convinced yet, here is little more truth from Investopedia.com.

This industry is projecting total revenues greater than $24B in 2015. Most of the total sales is beer at about 42%

followed by 31% of distilled beverages, and the rest, about 27% is made up of food and other items.

Investing in this type of business may be a great idea, but it's not for everyone; not everyone is cut out to own and operate such an establishment. It takes a certain type of personality and willingness to own and operate such a business to see great success.

There is much that goes into starting and owning your own trendy bar or nightclub. In this book, we are first going to look at what you can expect from owning a bar or nightclub and then if you still decide it is for you, then you can continue reading to find a step-by-step process on how to start, run and grow your own successful bar or nightclub business.

WHO SHOULD OPEN A BAR?

There are many types of people in the restaurant/bar-owning world: those with prior culinary or bartending experience, and those who have absolutely no prior experience, and those who are other business owners. People who have experience in the restaurant or bar world know how to mix a drink, how to serve or have an idea of how a restaurant is run, but have never owned their own business. You may fall into this category if you already have a clear vision for your menu or experience working in a bar, even if you have never assisted in the operation of such an establishment.

While having already worked the food business to some degree will give you an advantage in the exploration process of opening a trendy bar, there is still a considerable amount of market research that must be conducted to determine whether your bar concept will be a success or not.

Perfecting the most delicious death- by- chocolate Martini isn't going to guarantee that your business will turn a profit when your drink or food quality, service, and price are not correctly evaluated. There is a significant amount of research that is required before securing a location for your business and opening your doors.

You may not have any prior experience in the food and beverage industry, which is not necessarily a bad thing. Like me, you can have a great passion for mixing drinks at home and a dream of running your own business, but know nothing about running a bar or a restaurant and working with food or drinks.

The people who fall into this category may have a great deal of business knowledge and know what trends are on the rise in the business sector. With the right tools and guidance, people who fall into this group can profitably own and operate a small bar. When I first started exploring the idea of opening my own place, I was in this category. I knew the business world and language; running a bar was just like running any other successful company in many regards.

However, I still needed to learn about the people I would be serving, the brand I would be representing, and the process of building it all into a successful business.

Owning a business may sound fun and even easy to some people; after all, you will be your own boss and get to decide how much time you get off from work and can sample as many cocktails as you want.

A lot of people who enjoy bartending believe that they should start their own bar/tavern business. However, running any sort of bar or restaurant requires more than just serving customers and mixing a good margarita.

WHAT TO EXPECT WHEN STARTING A BAR/NIGHTCLUB

A successful bar/nightclub can easily be in the black within the first six months of opening, and even recover initial investment within three to five years. However, as with most businesses; the statistics for bars/nightclubs aren't in favor of the new startups. The main reason most new bars/nightclubs fail is because of a lack of capital to keep the business running. Another major reason is a lack of knowledge about the business, I can't help with the first reason, but I can minimize the second risk factor by offering you all the tips and advice you will need to start your new bar.

Bars are unlike restaurants when a new eatery place opens up; everyone wants to try their food out as soon as possible, so most new restaurants see a huge surge in business for the first three months then things die down. On the other hand, bars and taverns are opposite. As you first open, not many people will even notice you exist. So, the first three months are the toughest.

In this three months, your only focus is advertising and letting people know that you are there. So if you are thinking about opening a bar, you should also consider adding some funds in your budget to survive this hurdle. As I just mentioned, some new bars fall on their faces within the first 3-6 months because they didn't incorporate this cost into their long-term budget.

There are two types of people that start this business; the first type is the ones that are truly hands-on, they run, manage and operate their own bars. The other types are those who hire qualified people to run and operate the business on their behalf, and they just monitor the operation. In most cases, these are the people who either have other businesses or have a job that they are busy doing.

So, it is important to understand that just because you own a bar/nightclub, it doesn't necessarily mean you have to run it. If you'd rather, you can choose a team of good, trustworthy managers and you can start with them making the actual business work.

However, no matter what decision you make to run the business, you are going to have to be involved in the beginning. This means you need to be able to talk to people. If you are the type of person who wants to deal with paperwork instead of people then this business probably isn't for you. Getting to know your patrons and talking to people is an important part of customer service.

Another important thing to consider is the commitment of time and hours of operation. If you like getting up early in the morning, then you may not like the idea of owning a bar/nightclub that is open until three or four in the morning. If you have a family, it is important to consider how owning a bar/nightclub can affect family life as well. While you may be able to turn a lot of the work over to managers, it can easily take up to six months to reach this point, and this can cause some problems along the way.

If you still think starting a new bar/nightclub is the right thing for you then let's keep going. I am going to take you through all the steps needed to start your bar/nightclub and offer you some tips and advice to make it easier.

PROFITABILITY

As already mentioned, small-business and startups do not typically make a profit within the first year of opening. So, how long will it take for your business to turn a profit? This is one of the most common questions asked by new business owners. Money is a great concern for aspiring entrepreneurs, as many leave a well- paying career to take a chance on a risk that may not pay off.

The truth is that the answer is different for everyone. There is no guarantee when it comes to making money with a new small business. But, with my help and a lot of research, your chances will definitely increase.

Profitability depends on many factors, especially when it comes to the F&B (Food & Beverage) industry. It can also mean different things to different people. According to the technical definition, profit is when your revenues surpass your expenses, thus resulting in a profit. However, there is a difference between profit and making money. The term "ramen profitability" is when you are barely making enough money from your business to live.

For example, even if your bar is profitable after two months with $3,000 after expenses, don't expect to be able to live off that, but instead put it in savings. So, even turning a small profit does not mean that your business has succeeded. Your objective should not be to make enough to cover your living expenses but to pass the point of corporate profitability.

"Corporate profitability" is when you have excess remaining capital after all of your business and personal expenses have been paid. Often small business owners do not include themselves on the payroll. That is a mistake many new business owners make, but you must remember your own salary is part of your new business. Talk to your accountant, figure out a way to include yourself either on the payroll or "monthly draw" as a corporate officer of your business. The benefit of "monthly draw" is you pay less in social security tax and at the end of the year, your accountant issues a K-1 for your draws.

But don't take my advice as I am not a professional when it comes to taxes, seek real advice from a CPA or an accountant.

SETTING THE FOUNDATION

Your next question may be, "How do I get to corporate profitability?" Many startups have issues finding lenders or investors to source a small business loan because many will require evidence of corporate profitability first. The first step to achieving this is for your bar to break even every month. Reaching this goal means that you can finally stop investing your savings into the bar because it begins paying for itself. Once you have attained this milestone status, every dollar you earn will officially be considered profit.

However, there are many twists and turns that arise when starting a business, and you should account for every unexpected expense that may delay your break-even status. To calculate the bar's break-even point, you need to assess the gross profit after sales. Then subtract the staff and supplies costs, as well as your fixed and variable costs for the bar.

Gross Profit – Calculating your gross profit is simple and crucial when assessing a business at its revenue potential. Gross income is the total revenue accumulated by the cost of goods sold.

Net Profit – Your net profit is a good indicator of your business's financial health. Net income typically needs two crucial context indicators: industry knowledge/experience and the bar's net income trends anticipated based on past months. Ideally, you would like to see your net income increase over time to reach the compared net profit of other competitors in your sector.

Fixed Costs – Within the first few months of opening your bar, it will be difficult to calculate your fixed expenses. A fixed expense does not change with the goods and services produced. The salary of your employees, the location's rent, etc. remain the same regardless of how much you sell.

Variable Costs – After the initial surge of business from the grand opening, your foot traffic and sales will dwindle (as I mentioned earlier, first three months are the hardest). This means that the number of supplies and inventory will get smaller to meet the expected needs of clients and customers. The volume of goods produced will determine whether your variable expenses will increase or decrease.

BREAK-EVEN POINT

Once you know the bar's gross profit after sales cost and the fixed and variable expenses, you will be able to calculate how much the business needs to bring in to break even. Break-even point is where the sales are equal to the expenses. There is no profit and no loss. It is important that you know your break-even point. To calculate your break-even point simply use this formula below.

Break-Even Point = <u>Fixed Costs</u> ÷ <u>Gross Profit Margin Percentage</u>

For example, if your fixed expenses are $4,000 a month and you generate a twenty- five percent gross profit percentage, you will multiply $4,000 by 0.25 to calculate $16,000. This is what you will need to earn in sales to break even. There are several online break-even calculators that can help you break down the math to better understand the equation.

LOOKING TOWARDS THE FUTURE

A pro-forma income statement will help you determine when your business will break even. Pro-forma income lays out a financial statement with hypothetical estimates to create a picture of your business's profits based on data used if certain non-recurring expenses were not included in the analysis.

Pro-forma estimates are not calculated using generally accepted accounting principles (GAAP) and disregard one-time costs that are not part of the bar's normal operations. A pro-forma statement requires four components: sales projections, costs, additional expenses, and a gross estimate. The end result will give you a picture of when you can expect to break even.

1. Sales Projections: As you begin putting together your business plan and after your first year of operation, you will need to determine a hypothetical estimate of how many sales your bar will make every month for the first 1-3 years. This will require a lot of research and the knowledge that you build about your business sector to generate a budget of expected sales.

2. <u>Cost of Goods and Valued Services</u>: The drinks that you plan on making and selling will need a cost of goods sold budget report to determine the overall expected expenses needed to fulfill your bar's needs. You will also need to take into account the salaries of your employees.

3. <u>Additional Expenses</u>: Sometimes new business owners make the mistake of not accounting for all the little expenses that will factor into the overall projection of cost and required funding. When creating your pro-forma(a realistic projection), you will need to include additional expenses, like rent, internet, website building and maintenance, phone, insurance, debt repayments, accounting and bookkeeping costs, and utilities. Add your other expenses together to total your monthly fixed expenses.

4. <u>Gross Profit Estimate</u>: Once you have the information listed above, you will be able to determine when your bar will become profitable. Use the sales projections to figure out how many goods you will sell during a set period of time, and then subtract your expenses to determine an

estimate of the gross earnings. Making a month-to-month report of the additional expenses, costs of goods and services, and sales projections and making a visual display via chart will give you a clear picture of what point in time your bar will become profitable.

RESTAURANTS BY THE NUMBERS

If you want to run any F&B (Food & Beverage) company, you need to put into perspective the most important costs for your business. Ingredients, supplies, and labor costs are known as "prime costs" in the food industry. If you are capable of comparing these expenses in a percentage format against hypothetical scenarios that may arise during your years of operation will be helpful in the management of your bar.

It is often difficult to determine your costs in comparison to other food businesses because expenses vary widely per type of establishment. Food (mostly alcohol in this case) and labor costs will be different for the different types of foodservice operations. Luxurious establishments will have higher costs than a casual diner, for example.

The product sales combined with the quality of ingredients, pricing on the menu, and hours of operation will factor into your food and service cost percentages. You also may need to take into account the state minimum wage and differences in tip credit allowances. Although a small bar will not require wait staff, you should still consider how your cashiers and kitchen staff (in the event you are offering some snack menu in your bar) will be compensated and take it into account.

30-20 Rule

Most restaurants and fast foods live by a rule of thumb called the 30-20 rule. 30-20 is essentially the food and labor cost which are the two biggest expenses in the retail food industry. A general guideline for the industry is that the food cost should not exceed 30% of the sales and the labor should be within 20% of the sales.

But bar business defies that. It stays far below this rule. Bars don't sell expensive prime cut steaks or Alaskan snow crab legs. They mostly sell various mixed drinks and a few snacks like wings, mozzarella sticks, nachos and such. So, as for the cost, the most expensive item or ingredient in the bar is the actual alcohol. All the rest are water, juice or other drink mixes. As for snacks, none of these snack items are prime cut steaks, so they are relatively cheap and not very labor intensive to fry or bake.

Here is a simple calculation. Any typical 750 liquor bottle has almost 26 oz. of liquor. Most drinks you order at a bar comes with one ounce of alcohol unless you ask for a double shot. So let's say a bottle of 750 ml Smirnoff vodka may cost you around $22 in retail stores with which you can make 25 single drinks. Now let's say for a Vodka with Cranberry or a Screwdriver (Vodka and Orange Juice) you charge $7.50, which is the very typical mid-range price for such drinks across the country. Let's multiply $7.50 X 26 Oz = $195 is what you will earn from that single bottle.

Let's now analyze how much each of this drinks cost to make.

Each ounce of this Smirnoff vodka was 0.84 cents, the cranberry or orange juice was another 0.15 cents, Ice, straw and the napkin all combined was another 0.05 cents. So the grand total is $0.84 + $0.15 + $0.05 = $1.04. But your selling price was $7.50, so your gross profit on this sale was $7.50 - $1.04 = $6.46 which is not bad would you agree? Since this is very important for you to understand the pour cost and how it can impact your ultimate profitability, I will discuss this more later in the book.

As for labor, most bars do not have wait staff, so the labor is lower than most fast food and other fast-casual restaurants as well. You may hire a couple of kitchen staff and maybe one or two bartenders. Depending on how you run your bar, you may find out that your F&B cost will never go over 10-14% and your labor should never go over 15%. Thus, you are surpassing 90% of other food chains in profitability. So, your chance of success is far greater than most other food retailers.

Some fast food establishments may have labor costs as low as twenty- five percent, while restaurants with table service will experience labor within the thirty to thirty-five percent range. Similarly, food costs, including beverages, will fall between twenty- five to thirty- eight percent range, depending on the type of restaurant and varying sales.

This may sound like a lot of information, but remember that it is the experience of food and service that really makes a difference when it comes to the bottom line.

The finances are just one small part of what it takes to run a successful bar, and you shouldn't let it scare you away from opening your dream location!

FINDING MONEY FOR YOUR STARTUP

To start any business, the first thing you will need is access to money. I am sure you know that, but the question is how. Here are some ideas.

SIX WAYS TO FIND MONEY FOR YOUR BAR BUSINESS

There are few ways to go about finding the required funds.

1. Your own savings/401K etc.
2. A home equity line of credit (this is how I got started with mine)

3. Family funding (where your parents, siblings help you with a personal loan)
4. Create a partnership with people that have the money
5. Crowdfunding
6. Applying for a small business loan at your local bank

Sit down, take a piece of paper, try to analyze each and every option, and then see which one seems more doable for you. You can even do a mix and match here. For example, you need $100,000 to open your bar business, but you only have $50,000. One idea is to ask one or two like-minded friends or family to come in as a 50% partner, where you hold 50% of the business, the other two gets 25% each.

As for crowdfunding, I have never done it, but have seen people do it. You can make a list of 10-20 people that you know. Ask each of them for an investment of $10,000 for a 7% stake in your company. If 10 of them agree, you will have $100,000, and you only gave out 70% of your business. The remaining 30% is still yours for FREE.

You just have to be creative, remember when there is a strong will power to achieve something, there is always a way to get there.

Applying for a loan at the bank is the hardest of all other methods I outlined above. In the event you have no other option but to apply for a loan, you do have to do some research first.

First come up with a list of banks you want to apply to, it is not a good idea to apply at multiple banks at once, instead come up with a list of say four banks. Visit with them and talk in depth with their business loan department and find out if that bank offers loans for your type of projects, there are banks that do not offer loans for restaurants.

In my experience, typically smaller local banks are more inclined to offer loans to local family-owned bakeries, restaurants, coffee shops, and another similar type of businesses than some of the bigger banks. But that may not be true for every part of the country, so it is best to talk to at least 3-4 banks and try to get the feel if they are really into these sort of business financing or not before you submit your application.

Sometimes your local business brokers or commercial real estate agents can guide you to the right bank as they often deal with similar situations. They know which banks are more favorable to these sort of loans. You can also ask your bank that you deal with every day and ask for their advice.

Once you narrow down to say two banks, pay each of them a visit, have a meeting with their loan officer and see what their requirements are. Just remember every bank will have similar requirements, but they can vary widely based on many factors, such as how much down payment they require, how much collateral they will need from you. They may still need this information if they offer some SBA assisted loans.

Your goal would be to deal with a bank that offers SBA loans. SBA stands for Small Business Administration. This is where federal government guarantees part of your loan to the bank.

Most times SBA offers some sort of guarantee(typically 50-80%) on your behalf to the bank, so banks are somewhat more lenient in approving the loan as they are at lower risk for the total amount they loan you. But the downside to this is the amount of paperwork you have to furnish. It is monumental.

SBA's requirements can be broad and extensive, so be prepared to gather up a lot of paperwork.

Another drawback to SBA loan is it can take up to 4 months to get approval from them as they run slower than most banks. In their defense, they do have a lot of applicants that are submitting applications, which is always first come first serve, so be patient.

But if you have larger down payment (30% or higher) or have some good collateral to offer, then you can opt out on SBA loans and get most any bank to provide you a conventional business loan. Provided you have all your ducks in a row like your credit is in excellent shape, your tax returns show good incomes for previous years and so on.

When you talk to any banks, they will hand you something called a loan package, most times the package will have a checklist of documents that you need to furnish them, along with a loan application and some other waiver forms depending on your bank.

One thing to keep in mind, all banks and commercial lenders do have to follow certain guidelines that are set by federal and state banking authorities. Also, every bank will look at something call LTV (Loan to Value) ratio of the property or business you are looking to buy. LTV is essentially where banks look at the actual value of the business you are wanting to buy or lease and how much of that value they can loan you.

Let's look at the list of documents you will need to get ready to submit to your bank. Some of these items I will mention here may not be on your bank's checklist but do gather them anyway as it will make you look more professional and business-like.

11 Documents You Need for Loan Application

1. You need to get copies of at least last three years of personal tax returns, make sure the copies are signed.

2. Your resume (they may not even ask you for it, but remember the person that may approve your loan may never meet you but this way at least he or she gets to see who you are and how qualified you are.)

3. Copy of your Corporation Articles, (yes you have to get this done before you even apply for your loan, I will touch on how to file a corporation in the next chapter)

4. Personal financial statement for all Corporation Officers or members, make sure to sign it, if you are married and file joint tax returns than your wife needs to have one prepared for her as well or you can make a joint personal financial statement for both of you and make sure to both sign that document.

5. Copy of the commercial appraisal (in the event you are buying a location instead of leasing).

6. Copy of signed purchase agreement and Letter of Intent (in the event you are buying an existing bar).

7. Copy of your EIN (Employer's Identification Number) issued by the IRS.

8. Copy of all member/partner's Driver's licenses and social security cards.

9. A well thought out and expertly written Business Plan (not a store bought one or copy-pasted one, but one that is written for your specific business. Get some help if you

need to, as this has to be a well thought out plan. Fo it as if your life depends on it-trust me on this.)

10. Last but not the least is the loan application all filled out. Use a computer and printer if possible, if not write very clearly, so it is easy to read.

11. A cover letter addressed to the loan department where you describe what is in the package and thanking them for reviewing your loan application. Lastly, tell them where they can easily reach you if they need further help or other documents from you. It just makes you look more professional.

Now, remember to organize these papers with nice tabs and in a binding folder where anyone can open the folder, looking at the tabs, they can go directly to that specific section.

If you are applying for an SBA specific business loan, then SBA may also give you a loan package with some more documents and forms to fill out, but they will mostly ask for the same as I just mentioned.

But yes they will have you fill out many more forms, and you do not have to visit the SBA office as they work through your local banks so the loan officer you deal with will furnish you all of that.

Now, let's take a look at the estimated cost of opening a typical bar business

ESTIMATED COST OF OPENING A BAR IN A SMALL TO MID-SIZE CITY

ITEMS	COST
Lease Deposit, Insurance & License Fees	$3,500 - $35,000
Build out/Layout	$10,500 - $85,000
Equipment Décor & Furniture(New or used)	$25,000 - $70,000
Counter Top & Display Shelving (For Liquor)	$7,500 - $15,000
Lighting, Signage & Music System ***	$7,500 - $25,000
POS, Credit Card & Video Equipment	$4,500 - $7,500
Initial Inventory	$18,000 - $33,500

Employee Training & Uniform	$1,500
Startup Cash	$5,000
TOTAL:	**$83,000 - $277,500**

*** If you are opening a club and not a bar, assume the music/speaker system to cost on the high side of this estimate.

ESTIMATED MONTHLY EXPENSES

ITEMS	COST
Utilities	$2,000 - $3,000
Rent/Mortgage	$3,500 - $8,000
Payroll (Including Taxes)	$4,500 - $7,000
Maintenance & Repair	$500 - $1,000
Insurance (BOP) ***	$750 - $1,500
Legal and Licenses	$250 - $500
Accounting & Bookkeeping	$150 - $350

Supplies	$250
Misc. Expenses	$500
TOTAL:	$12,400 - $22,100

***BOP or Business Owner's Policy insurance premium can vary widely depending on your location, your city, and state.

ESTIMATED MONTHLY INCOME CALCULATION

Take a look at this P&L (Profit & Loss) statement.

DIRTY MARTINI

Profit and Loss Statement
Dec-17

Revenue:	**Sales $**
Liquor & Wine Sales	$17,852.00
Draft Beer Sales	$4,152.25
Pre Pkgd Beer Sales	$2,722.98
Food Sales	$6,454.45
Private Party Sales	$3,250.00
Gross Revenue	**$34,431.68**
Cost of Goods Sold $	
Liquor Sales	$2,859.35
Draft Beer Sales	$1,674.36
Pre Pkgd Beer Sales	$852.19
Food Sales	$1,542.85
Private Party Sales	$1,790.21
Total COGS	$8,718.96
Gross Profit:	**$25,712.72**
Store Expenses:	
Payroll	$6,715.10
Utility	$2,341.55
Rent	$4,160.00
Advertising	$772.00
Insurance	$859.00
C.C. Charge	$294.10
Maintenance	$309.00
License &Mics	$150.00
Security	$100.00
Accounting	$125.00
Misc.	$150.00
Total Expense	$15,975.75
Net Profit:	**$9,736.97**

Now before you dispute these numbers, remember these are real good faith estimates. These number may vary widely depending on if you are trying to open your new bar in New York City or Tuscaloosa, AL.

KNOWING THE MARKET AND SETTING A TREND

Let's take a break from money- talk and center our focus on a much more fun topic: choosing a concept for your bar! You may already have some great ideas planned out, which is a good jumping- off point in getting started. Unfortunately, some themes and ideas are better on paper or do not coincide with what is trending in the current market.

There are many types of restaurant concepts to consider, and of course, you want your bar to stand out from the rest! But before you decide on a specific idea, there are several questions that you need to consider:

- Who is your target clientele?
- What is the price range of your drinks?
- Where will your establishment fall on the scale of formal to casual?
- Is there one item on your menu that you would like to build your brand around?

When I first started planning my bar, I was almost completely set on branding my entire business on just hard liquor, but then I started visiting a few bars in nearby bigger cities and realized that there are so much more to offer in a trendy bar then just scotch on the rocks.

After a lot of market research on the customers in my city and competing shops, I found that my idea wasn't the best path for my business to build on. Your bar's design theme can include a few different concepts, merging ideas to make your shop unique. Just because you feel set on an idea doesn't mean it is the best for your business. Take your time to really look into what will make your bar business successful for the long-term. Here are a few examples of new and trendy concepts that you should keep in mind as you decide the kind of bar that you want to run, and how it may fit into your ideal location.

One of the biggest concepts trending right now is the fast-casual establishment. This trend is a bit more upscale than most typical bars (those with pool and foosball tables).

Instead think of trendy as modern love seats, couches, and chairs. A piano on the corner. Some beautiful yet clever lighting everywhere and the sound of Martini shakers at the bar. A place where people come after work to have a beer or a martini and hangout. Maybe they can get a bite of snacks with their drinks too.

LIMITING YOUR THEME OPTIONS BY ELIMINATION

There are many different routes that your bar can take, and I'm sure that most of your ideas have the potential to truly succeed in the casual F&B industry. But, the reality is that you don't have the means to test all of them out before settling on the one that works best. However, there are a few ways that you can at least limit your ideas to the ones that are most likely to exceed in your location and present market.

- Keep an Eye on the Competition: Take a look at the bars that are already doing well in your area. What types of establishments do you see around you? Are there a lot of 80's style bars, where they have pool tables? Are there any bars based on any themes? Is another bar already known for their dirty martinis or margaritas? If your bar isn't different from those that are already established in your area, how will your concept stand out from the rest? Study your competitors and learn as much as you can about their pricing, menu, theme, and customer relations. Even if you do not like a specific bar, find out why others do.

- Decide How Much You Want to Spend on Your Theme: Let's be honest, most of us do not have the money to play around with different themes and concepts. When starting a new bar, there usually isn't a lot of wiggle room to waste money on décor just to change it a few weeks later when your opinion has changed. Opening a bar is not cheap, but you also don't want to compromise on the theme that will brand your business. Some concepts will cost more than others to create.

- <u>Keep Your Focus</u>: When I was seventeen, I worked at a restaurant that functioned as a café during the day, and an Italian restaurant at night. The owner even went as far as changing the layout of the dining room to transition the establishment from one concept to the other. This wasn't only confusing for the staff, but also for potential customers. People that were coming through the area while traveling didn't understand the website and didn't respond well to the constantly changing arrangement.

Fads come and go, but that doesn't mean your business should always be trying to keep up with the hottest trends. Attempting to fit the ever-changing needs or desires of the marketplace will compromise your bar's identity and potentially run the business out of money. This isn't to say that you shouldn't try a new drink, food or snack menu.

Just stay true to your concept and focus your brand on strengthening it.

NAMING YOUR BAR

One of the most important factors that play into the overall branding of your bar is the name. Making the transition from bartending as a hobby to making it an official business is an exciting adventure that serves a snappy and catchy name to go with it.

Choosing a name is a fun part of starting a business and should be a relaxing break from forming a business plan and budgeting. Here are a few helpful do and don't tips that will hopefully inspire you to choose the perfect name for your bar.

DO'S

- Make it clear that your business is a bar. This may sound like an obvious statement, but often new business owners overlook naming a business specifically about that niche; choosing broader names instead of alcoholic beverage-related titles. For example, a bar called "Cathy's Pit Stop" is too general, making it more difficult for people to find online. It may also lead to assumptions that the shop is for artists, crafters, or hobby enthusiasts.

Changing the name to "Cathy's Brewing House" will make it easier for people to find the bar online when searching, and makes a statement of what Cathy specializes in, although the shop may offer more than just brewed beer. This doesn't mean that you should use the straightforward word "bar" in your company's name, but that you should at least consider referencing martini, beer, brewer or even the word bar in the name (Cathy's Martini Bar).

- Give your business room to grow. You do not want to limit yourself by choosing a name that is too specific. For example, even if your bar's specialty is locally brewed beer, you don't want to call it "Cathy's Brew House." What if at a later point your bar becomes well known for its dirty martinis? You should always give leeway for your business to grow, when if you have a specific vision that you want to fulfill.

DON'TS

- Do not pick a name that has already been used by someone else. Even if your first name is Steve and you want your bar to specifically sell martinis, you should not name your business Steve's Martini Bar, because if it is already taken you can very well run into legal trouble. Regardless, if you are halfway across the country, resist the temptation to name a business with something that has already been taken. Using a name that is already in use will also make it difficult to claim a URL for the website, make a Facebook page and Twitter handle, etc. You don't want to confuse customers by competing with a bar that has the same name as yours.

OTHER CONSIDERATIONS

Family Names are often safe to use, but can sometimes be boring. Using your last name is not necessarily the most creative strategy for naming your bar, but it does add a sense of personal identity and familiarity in smaller communities.

Adding Obscure Words to your name can really confuse customers in what your shop is selling. Although it may seem fun and quirky to call your Martinis "Devilish" or "crooked," those who are less attuned to their home thesaurus will not know what to expect when walking into your bar.

Be Careful When Choosing Puns. In a world that is accustomed to internet memes and constant wordplay, choosing to use a pun in your bar name is not always the wisest idea. Although it may be hard to believe, some people do not enjoy puns and find that they grow stale quickly. Punny names can isolate some customers who do not find them cute or amusing. If you are playing with some ideas that involve wordplay, consider how embarrassing or overused it will be every time you answer the phone. This is a good indicator of whether the pun is appropriate or not.

Don't be Overly Cute with Spelling. This may coincide with using puns in your shop's name, but you should also consider the possible negative outcomes that may arise from using cutesy spelling in your business's name. For example, "Kat's Kute Martini" may be difficult for customers to find online because the spelling is quirky. If clients do not already know how to spell your company's name just by hearing it, then how are they going to find your business?

BRAINSTORM: FORMULAS FOR TRYING NEW CREATIVE NAMES

If you are still having trouble finding the perfect name for your bar, consider using these simple formulas to spark those creative juices.

Object + Product

Examples: Rocket Donuts, Bluebell Ice Cream, Sticky Fingers Bar

Location + Product

Examples: Big Apple Cakes, Pacific Pastry Shoppe, Downtown Desserts

Baking- Related + the word "Bar."

Examples: Wooden Spoon Bar, Cookie Cutter Bar, Lick the Spoon Bar

PUTTING TOGETHER A BUSINESS PLAN

Now that you have your company's name and a concept in place, it's time to construct your business plan. Investors and banks will want to know how you plan on making your bar a success with a step-by-step analysis and list of factors that you have taken into consideration.

5 BIGGEST MISCONCEPTIONS ABOUT BUSINESS PLANS

No one ever told you about a business plan before

It's natural that many bar owners wouldn't have been exposed to the process of creating a business plan. While some businesses can succeed without one, it is not the suggested method of opening a business. The first thing you may want to familiarize yourself with the different points the business plan will highlight.

You are confused on where to start

So business owners may know think they need a business plan, but just may not understand where they need to start and they just decided not to do it. This is not ever a good idea. Every business owner has to begin at some point. You have to find a way to begin your business plan if you want to be able to use it to bring your dreams to life.

You think it is just too hard

Starting a business plan doesn't have to be difficult, but you have to put the work in. It also takes a large amount of thoughtfulness and time. While planning doesn't always guarantee success, not planning will almost definitely lead to failure. It may not seem like a fun thing to do, but losing all of your money because you didn't have one doesn't seem like fun either. To start your plan, you don't have to start from scratch. There are many online resources to get you started.

You think your business is too small to be worth the trouble

You might think that a business plan would be overkill because you are just starting one small business, but a small business would benefit from having a thoughtfully written business plan. Even small businesses have hundreds of things to keep track of and consider.

You think you can keep all the plans in your head

Sometimes business owners think that they should rely on their mental abilities or just their memories instead of taking the time to develop their business plan. But they are not considering when starting a business they will be way too busy working on the day-to-day operations to remember everything that they would need to do to open their business.

SIX COMPELLING REASONS YOU NEED A BUSINESS PLAN FOR YOUR BAR

YOUR BUSINESS PLAN WILL SAVE YOU MONEY

No matter how much you love the different types of vodka, gin or tequila related to making margaritas or martinis, it is important to remember that a bar is a business. Without having an organizational chart and estimate on profitability, your business will not succeed. So plan as much as possible in the beginning.

When you start any business, it is almost impossible not to go beyond the original budget estimates. Underestimating the expenses for a bar business is typical, even if you have a well formatted and thought-out business plan.

A way to avoid overspending and sticker shock is to anticipate your expenses accurately, then add 5 to 10 percent to that. Use this number as if you don't have a penny more. Don't buy what you don't need and can't afford. A business plan is a perfect place to have a written out plan of expenses. Also, if you have a business plan, it will help you consider the basic financial costs that anyone can easily overlook.

With this information, you should realize that if you do not have a written plan, you will more than likely spend much more money and waste a considerably larger amount of time because you have planned no way to manage the budget for your bar business effectively.

Your Business Plan Will Keep You Organized

Being organized saves money. This habit also saves business owners stress and headaches. A business plan can start your bar business off on the right foot. After creating a business plan, you would then know the pace of which things need to be started and the completion date of tasks

You can use your business plan as a general checklist. You have to be somewhat general, without all of the small details involved with completing your tasks. Choosing not to include too many details is important because you want your business plan to stay at a readable length. You want just enough information so that you and other people can read and understand the plan.

YOUR BUSINESS PLAN WILL KEEP YOU ON TRACK

It doesn't matter if you have one or a hundred businesses, there are always specific elements that you have to address in the initial steps in starting up your bar business.. So having a business plan will keep you on track, making sure that no tasks are left undone.

Remember that your business plan will be read by investors, banks, and stakeholders as well as your property manager.

When writing your plan, consider your audience. The document needs to be tailored to their requirements as well as your own. The audience for your business plan is pretty small, but very important. Your property manager will most likely want to see a business plan from you to make sure that you plan for their space will be beneficial to them as well as practical.

You might not be aware, but they might actually have a few different competing business proposals for their properties. Your business plan will need to be well thought out and articulate description of your vision and goals.

Because they are investing their money in you and your business, they want to assess their risk. Stakeholders and potential investors will want a well thought out business plan before choosing to invest.

YOUR BUSINESS PLAN WILL HELP YOU STAY ON COURSE

There will be quite a few important questions that will need to be answered in the planning phase of your bar business. A huge element of the planning phase will be spending considerable time figuring your budget. As spoken about previously, the financial projections are a large hurdle to get over.

Know that because it is difficult doesn't mean that you can avoid the task and just do a general overview. Not doing anything at all is one of the worst things you can do for your fledgling business. Start a habit of keeping excellent financial records, and staying close to your budget at all times. This is important, especially in the beginning.

Isn't Writing a Business Plan Difficult?

Writing a business plan certainly doesn't have to be hard. It is crucial to follow along with the process as closely as possible. Simplicity is the key. You have goals and dreams for your business, so your business plan turns all of those goals and dreams into an actual business. A real-life entity that you run. This is the first step to taking your goals and making them into a reality. Your business plan can be a written guideline for you to follow well past opening day. This will keep you close to your original goals and vision.

It is up to you how complex your business plan is. It is important to remember that you want to be able to come back to this document over and over again. This can end up wasting a lot of time if you have an unnecessarily lengthy document. You will avoid it instead of using it as the resource as it is. A complex document will not impress anyone.

It will also take time to thoroughly research, as well as solve, the potential problems that can arise when writing your business plan. The most important thing to remember is to remain positive and approach the task in a cool and calm manner.

You don't have to write your entire business plan in one afternoon. In fact, don't even try. Spend time brainstorming. Think about what exactly what you want and then plan the exact way that you will be able to achieve these goals.

Start with your overall goals. Then break each goal into one to three smaller goals and then go from theirs. Choose to see it as an opportunity for you to get those creative juices flowing. It's fun to figure out the wants and needs of your potential business.

The more positively you look at the process, the more likely it will be that you finish with a document that you feel is representative of your future business and yourself.

How Long Does a Business Plan Have to Be?

This is a kind of tough question to answer. The reason for this is the time length really depends on the individual and the individual business, and the complexity of the chosen concept. A good ballpark for a bar business plan should be anywhere from 7 to 15 pages once it's completed.

It can be even more depending on your needs for details. It might sound like it's a lot, but in reality, it's not. You should always use headings as well as subheadings. Also, space between paragraphs and sections are important for readability when constructing your business plan. This will also give you a place to write notes in the margins.

Here is a website that you can check out, they prepare custom business plans for various businesses once you provide them with enough data. I have used them before, and I can honestly say they do a great job.

http://BPlans.com

A business plan visualizes the market research you do, which shows that you understand the reasons customers will buy your goods. Market research examines consumer behavior, cultural and societal influence, and personal circumstances that influence customers in what they buy and do.

MARKET RESEARCH

Market research is separated into two categories to be studied: primary and secondary.

PRIMARY RESEARCH

Primary research analyzes customers candidly and directly. Examples of primary research are telephone interviews or online surveys from random samples within your target audience. After you have opened your bar, you can also use your own sales records to study how your products are being consumed by customers.

The objective of the primary research is to collect data from studying current trends, sales, and current effective strategies. Primary research will also allow you to consider your competitor's marketing plans to give you a clear picture of the practices that are failing and succeeding in your industry.

Examples of Primary Research

- In person or telephone interviews
- Surveys
- Focus groups
- Questionnaires

Sample Questions:

- What factors do you take into consideration when buying (your product)?

- What do you like/dislike about the products currently available right now?
- What do you think would improve these products and services?
- What is an ideal price for this product/service?

SECONDARY RESEARCH

Analyzes information that other people have gathered about consumers. Examples of secondary research are reports that can be found online or in published articles that are written by and for people within your industry. The objectives of the secondary research are to evaluate data that identifies your competitors, determine benchmarks, and recognize target segments. Target segments are the type of people who fall within the bar's target demographic.

When creating your business plan, you can include either category or even both. A business, no matter what industry it falls under, can't succeed without clearly understanding its consumers, goods, services, and the market overall. The business world is full of competitors, and each entrepreneur wants their business to succeed just as much as you do. Not doing the proper research and market analysis necessary to do well, will give your competitors an advantage.

A business plan is a conclusive document of answers to any question that may be asked when analyzing your business as a whole. A few examples of the questions that you should be trying to answer are:

- *Who are your target consumers?* Think of answering this question as if you were creating an avatar of your ideal customer. Describe their age, income, level of education, career, etc.

- *Where do your potential customers go right now?* This studies their habits and how your products will relate to their lifestyle. How much do they spend and buy? Study their usual suppliers and shops, favored price points, and the most popular goods right now.

- *What motivates them to go to a bar?* This question may be difficult to answer, as you have to think like a consumer and truly ponder what makes them buy things that they may not necessarily need but still want. A consumer may look to purchase the cookware that offers the most efficient nonstick solution, or may only buy the cheapest goods to get the best deal for their dollar. There are also consumers who routinely buy the same brands because they trust them, or only purchase goods that come in the greatest variety of decorative colors.

- *What will make consumers stop at your business?* There are hundreds of data that provide detailed information about the markets, consumer habits, and sales figures. Will it be the quality of your baked goods? Will your prices be reasonable for the median income earner? Is your bar going to offer a friendly atmosphere, or be designed to appeal to white-collar workers? There are many motivators to consider as you delve into the minds of your customers to understand why your shop is the ideal place for them to spend their hard-earned money.

When you take a look at all the sources of information to answer as many questions as possible about your business and the people who are most likely to purchase your beverage, it will give you a clearer vision on how to run your bar as well as make your odds of success greater and sound more appealing to investors. If you are unsure of how to design your business plan, there is online software (Bplan.com) that helps you utilize the information you gather during your research, as well as additional data that pertains to your business sector.

You want to add at least some of your own material, even if you use a program that was created by someone else who was looking to open a bar and made their business plan available to the public. You want your business to be different, better, and to stand on its own apart from the rest of your competitors.

Part of your business plan should include companies that will give you further information on your industry; include studies and reports on large and individual enterprises. There are professional businesses that will conduct in-depth market research for you, but it doesn't come cheap. Large businesses invest thousands upon thousands of dollars to research trends and data to create new ideas and marketing strategies to generate more income.

To conduct this research on your own, start by utilizing your social media accounts. Look at what your target consumers are liking and disliking on their pages, look at their ad preferences and what posts gather the greatest responses. Using Facebook and Google Analytics, you can easily read the numbers of your own online visitors on your bar's website.

Websites that encourage the average consumer to voice their opinions, values, and beliefs will offer you direct marketing insight into a customer's actions and thoughts in a cohesive way.

What Else Should be Included in Your Business Plan?

Making a business plan for your bar forces you to learn about the many aspects of the F&B industry, as well as give your dream a localized perspective in looking at the competition within your community and local economy. Additionally, a business plan is absolutely necessary for any new company that is looking for investors or another outside financing.

However, as you begin to gather all of this information, you may not know what to do with it! Creating a business plan sounds easy once you start putting your research together, but you want to look professional and organized by constructing a plan that is more than just random data. Take a look at this breakdown of all the essential parts of your bar's business plan.

1. <u>Executive Summary</u>

    An executive summary is an introduction to your bar, giving the reader a general overview of the entirety of the business plan. Get creative with your executive summary to keep it interesting, so that you do not lose your reader's interest. Within your summary, be sure to include:

    - The basics of your bar idea/concept. This should include the name, theme concept, style of bar, location, etc.

    - Why you are the best person to go into this business venture with. This is the time to give any background you have in bartending or business. You need to sell them on the idea that regardless of whether or not you have experience in the F&B industry, you are still the right person to open this unique bar.

2. Company Description

   This second piece of your business plan is also called a "business analysis." This gives the reader or investor a deeper insight into the type of bar you are going to open; expanding on the initial look, you gave in the executive summary. Within this part of the business plan, you should include:

   - The exact location of the bar
   - The name you chose
   - The style/theme of the bar
   - A sample menu
   - Local competitors
   - The population of the general area

3. Market Analysis

   This third part of a business plan is often referred to as the "marketing strategy." It shows your investors that you know your ideal consumer demographic and have done enough research to know how best to reach out and influence them. There are three parts to displaying a market analysis within a business plan.

- <u>Industry</u>: Who is your ideal customer? What times during the day would your business be busiest? Give a detailed explanation of your customer base and why they are going to choose to go to your bar over your competitor's.

- <u>Competition</u>: I cannot stress enough how important it is to know your competitors as well as you know your own business. It is often the competition that makes or breaks a new business; and if you are investing your own money, you can't afford to lose out. Companies that have been there for years already have a loyal fan base, making it more difficult for you to find customers. Take a paragraph or two to explain how you will compete with a business that is already well-known within the community.

- <u>Marketing</u>: What marketing strategies will you use to promote your bar? What methods will you practice to entice your core audience to stop and enjoy a drink at your place? Some examples of this include: offering early bird special, special price/drink offerings to local business professionals, giving a seniors' discount. How will your advertisements set you apart from competitors, and what will you specifically do to advertise your business?

- USP (Unique Selling Proposition): Last, but never the least, mention what your unique selling proposition is for your business. It is the very idea that has driven you to take the plunge to open your own bar. It could be that "there are no other piano bars in the area" or "there are no martini bars in the city."

Some other key elements you should include in your business plan are business operation details and management overviews. You should explain the exact hours of operation for your bar, how many employees you plan to hire, and restaurant vendors or local farms that will help with the food and beverage supply.

You should also describe how your bar will run, especially when you are not there. Who is going to manage the suppliers, employees, finances, etc.? In this part of the business plan, you should include who you plan on hiring and how they will be a great addition to your new bar.

LEGAL ASPECTS OF YOUR BUSINESS

In this chapter, we are going to dive into the legal aspect of creating your business. The good news is that you are already halfway there towards opening up your bar! Unfortunately, we have to go back to business-talk and the step-by-step process of franchising your business and filing for an LLC status.

As you continue to develop your brand and the best methods of creating a strong presence in your community, you will also have to do more to protect the name you have built for your bar. Your brand is your identity, and you do not want it to be compromised by another competitor stealing your concept.

INCORPORATING YOUR BUSINESS

1. Choose a name for your business that is not already in use and adheres to your state's filing rules. The office (typically the county probate court) that handles corporate article filing requests is usually within the same office as the corporation's sector in the secretary of state's office. Although the rules for naming a new company may differ from state to state, generally, the requirements are as follows:

    o Your business's name can't be the same as a business that is already established as a corporation.

    o If you are filing for an LLC status, the company's name must end with the LLC label, or an abbreviation of the title/ phrase "Limited Liability Company;" such as LLC, Ltd. Liability Company, or L. L. C.

- Your business's name can't contain specific words that are barred from your state. Often, such limitations will include bank, corporation, insurance, etc.

If you are struggling to create a name that is true to the concept of your bar, you can contact your state's Secretary of State's office to determine if your prospective name is available. It is imperative that your bar's name does not fall into violation of someone else's trademark. Once you have established a legal and unused name, you typically don't need to register the name with your state, as the articles of organization will automatically register your new business's name.

2. File the formal paperwork, also known as articles of organization, and pay the required filing fee. This may cost between $100.00 to $800.00, depending on the state that you live in. A disadvantage of creating a corporation, rather than a partnership or sole proprietorship, is having to submit a filing fee with the articles of organization documents. In nearly every state, the fees are

$100.00 or less. However, larger states like California will charge a yearly tax of $800.00 along with the required filing fee.

3. Form a corporate operating agreement. This document outlines the rights and responsibilities expected of the company's participants. You can create your own articles of organization as well, which generally requires you to fill in your business's full name, address, and name the owners of the operation.

   An operating agreement does not need to be submitted to the probate court and is typically not required by most state laws. However, it is absolutely necessary to create one for your own records. An operating agreement allows you to establish rules of the operation and ownership of your bar. The foundation for creating an operating agreement may include:

   - Each member's percentage in the bar
   - Each member/ owner's rights and responsibilities
   - How the profits will be distributed

- What happens when a partner/member wants to buy out their share

4. Some states will also ask you to publish a notification of your objective to form a Limited Liability Company. While this step is only required in a few states, publishing a notice for your bar is a great way to announce your new business. This notification must be published in a local newspaper several times over a term of a few weeks, followed by filing an affidavit of publication to the probate court.

Every business needs to have the proper license, permits and other authorizations to be able to perform its normal course of business. When you choose a legal entity for your bar business, there are two main factors to consider:

- What kind of legal protection umbrella you want
- The type of business model you intend to build

Often you have the option of choosing to file as a limited liability company or LLC, general partnership or even sole proprietorship. A sole proprietorship is the ideal business structure for someone starting a bar business, especially if it is a moderate start from your home. However, most prefer the benefits of an LLC.

If you plan to eventually expand your bar business to other locations or potentially online, then you definitely don't want to file as a sole proprietor. In this instance, you should definitely file as an LLC.

When you file as an LLC, you will be able to protect yourself from personal liability. This means that if anything goes wrong while operating your business then only the money you invested into the company is at risk.

This isn't the case if you file as a sole proprietor or a general partnership. LLCs are simple and flexible to operate since you won't need a board of directors, shareholder meetings or other managerial formalities in order to run your business.

Here are all the legal business structures you can choose from, it is best to get some advice from your CPA or accountant or an attorney.

LEGAL STRUCTURE OF YOUR BUSINESS

When starting a business, there are five different business structures you can choose from:

- Sole Proprietor

- Partnership

- Corporation (Inc. or Ltd.)

- S Corporation

- Limited Liability Company (LLC)

SOLE PROPRIETOR

This is not the safest structure for bar business. It is used for a business owned by a single person or a married couple. Under this structure, the owner is personally liable for all business debts and may file their personal income tax. Not to mention the personal exposure you get from all the potential liabilities.

PARTNERSHIP

If your business is owned and operated by multiple people, when it comes to structuring your business, you can choose one of two kinds of partnerships. These two kinds of partnerships are general partnerships and limited partnerships.

In a general partnership, the partners manage the business together and are responsible for each other's debts. A limited partnership actually has both limited and general partners.

The general partners work as previously described, but the limited partners are only investors that don't actually have any control over the company and are not responsible for the debts in the same way.

CORPORATION (INC. OR LTD.)

The corporate structure is complex and costs quite a bit more money than most other business structures. This is because a corporation is a completely independent legal entity. It is separate from its owners. It also requires you to comply with more regulations and requirements.

A corporation provides increased liability protection for the business owner or owners. A corporation's debt is not considered that of its owners. This lessens your personal risk.

It isn't a very common structure among bars since there are shares of stocks involved.

Profits are taxed both at the corporate level and distributed to shareholders. When you structure a business at this level, there are often lawyers involved.

S CORPORATION

This is one of the most popular types of business entity people form to avoid double taxation. It is taxed similarly to a partnership entity. But an S Corp. needs to be approved to be classified as such, so it isn't very common among bar business.

The S corporation is going to be a more attractive option for small-business owners than a regular corporation. That's because an S corporation takes some great parts of what a corporation offers on a smaller, less expensive scale. It has some very appealing tax benefits as well as provides business owners with the liability protection of a corporation.

You have a couple of choices when it comes to filing the necessary paperwork for your business. The first is to have a lawyer or accountant to file a legal business entity for you.

You can also do it yourself using online resources, or by going to your local city office and filling out the necessary paperwork. You can go on websites like legalzoom.com and draw up the document for less money than what an attorney would charge to do the same.

LIMITED LIABILITY COMPANY (LLC)

This is the most common business structure among bar business. It offers benefits for small businesses since it reduces the risk of losing all your personal assets in case you are faced with a lawsuit. It provides a clear separation between business and personal assets. You can also elect to be taxed as a corporation, which saves you money come tax time.

If you are unsure which specific business structure you should choose then, you can discuss it with an accountant.

They will direct you to the best possible option for what your business goals are.

I filed my first LLC via Legalzoom.com as I didn't have the extra funds to hire an attorney. Thankfully, it worked out well for me. But my advice is, if possible, and you have the funds, do seek legal advice from an attorney or from your CPA before deciding on this matter.

APPLYING FOR AND OBTAINING AN EIN

EIN or Employer's Identification number is a unique 9 digit number that is issued by the IRS to each and every business. Think of this as the social security number for your business. Without this number, you can't own or operate a business with any of the legal corporate status, but you are choosing to go as a sole proprietor, then your social security number will be enough for you own and operate your business.

1. Determine Your Eligibility

- You can apply for an EIN online if your bar is located within the U.S. or a U.S. Territory.

- The person requesting an EIN needs to have an authentic Taxpayer Identification Number, such as a social security number or individual taxpayer identification number.
- You are restricted to one EIN per responsible party per day. A responsible party is defined as the person who controls or manages the business and the distribution of its money and assets.

2. For the Online Application...
- When you fill out an EIN application online, you have to complete it in one session, as it cannot be saved and returned to later.
- As you fill out the application, your session on the webpage will expire if you exceed 15 minutes of inactivity.

3. Submitting Your Application...

- After you have completed your application, submit it immediately to validate your business's status. You will receive validation and a confirmation notice. It is important to print and save your EIN confirmation as evidence that you filed as an employer.

Here is a link to IRS website where you can download or fill out the form online.

https://www.irs.gov/businesses/small-businesses-self-employed/how-to-apply-for-an-ein

OPENING A COMMERCIAL BANK ACCOUNT

This is one important step, but it can only be done after you have a fully executed article of incorporation which has been approved by the state, and you have an EIN assigned by the IRS.

Once you have these two documents, you should be able to go to a bank and open your first commercial bank account.

But remember to check and understand various types of commercial checking account fees, you want to find a bank that offers free or almost free commercial checking account because some larger banks can charge you hundreds of dollars each month depending on how many transactions you do. Make sure to ask and shop around before you sign on the dotted line.

CITY & COUNTY LICENSES & PERMITS

Since you are opening an F&B retail business, one of the most essential steps in your licensing process should be to discuss your proposed plan and operation with your local county health department and state liquor licensing authority. As they will be the ultimate authorities to issue you a food and liquor permit with which you can operate your business.

Next step would be to go to your local city and county business licensing office and find out what type of business and regulatory licenses you are required to have. It should take a few days to get your licenses and permits in place, and then you are finally and officially in business.

You also need to attend a 4-6 hour class to obtain your ServSafe permit. This is a certificate that ensures that the manager or the owner of any food-related businesses knows how to handle food safely.

Each establishment needs to have minimum of one person who is certified in the ServSafe program

Here is the link to ServSafe site so you can find out more about how to attend their class and get certified.

https://www.servsafe.com/

Local Laws

Local laws ensure that you are operating a fair and safe restaurant. Exact rules and enforcement differ from city-to-city and state-to-state.

Health Department
Govern what you eat, serve.
Sanitary rules for food safety and Sanitation parameters.
Good for one year at a time.
Can be revoked at any time.
State and local Health Departments work together Administering inspections and licenses.

Fire Department
Issues fire permits.
State fire marshal and local fire department administer regulations and Guidelines.
Must follow the National Fire Protection

Code.

Building Department
Issues building permits.
Performs inspections.
Building codes differ within Communities.
May have to deal with several building permits and occupancy Certificates.

ADDITIONAL AGENCIES TO CONFORM WITH

Signage Commission	Controls features of signage and permits.

Water and Sewer Commission	Determines septic system rules and water supply guidelines.

Americans with Disabilities Act (ADA)	Checks that disability and wheelchair requirements are met.

Dairy Commission	Often operates within the Health Department.

U.S. Department of Agriculture Department of Homeland Security	Regulate safety of food supplies.

Secretary of State	Must approve and register your business name.

LIQUOR LICENSE

TYPES OF LIQUOR LICENSES

Many are not aware that there are different types of liquor licenses as well. For example, most states have special licenses for exclusive-use clubs such as country clubs, restaurants, and bars so they can serve beer and wine.

License types vary widely between states, but most of the states offer two main types of liquor licenses.

1. On-Premises consumption

2. Off premises consumption

On-premises is for restaurants, bars, clubs and those types of establishments where off-premises licenses are for grocery stores, gas stations and other such retail stores where you can buy your alcohol but cannot consume on the premises.

There is another distinction between various liquor licenses in most states, and that is the level of license you get. For example, in Alabama, the State ABC (Alabama Beverage Control) board issues one type of license for just beer and wine sales, and a separate type of license to sell liquor.

So, it is best to start with your state's Liquor license board and find out their exact requirements before you go too far into planning your new bar.

LIQUOR LICENSE APPROVAL DIFFICULTIES

Even if you need to get a liquor license for your nightclub, the approval process can sometimes take up to a year. For example, in Los Angeles County you are required to notify 1,500 residents of your intent to open a nightclub that sells alcohol and then the county needs to hold a public assembly to approve your business.

Sometimes it can be a good idea to talk with a licensed business broker in your area who specializes in alcohol licenses. It can also be a good idea to hire a lawyer to help guide you through the process of applying for a liquor license. Lastly, you may just consider buying a liquor license from an existing establishment while you buy your building as well.

HOW TO GET A LIQUOR LICENSE

Anytime you want to start a business that involves the sale of alcohol; you need to get a liquor license. State and county liquor permits can range from $239 to a couple of thousand dollars. You'll need to submit an application and meet regulations set by the state and/or county in order to get approved for a liquor license. The process can take up to a year so make sure you use the following steps to increase your chances of getting approved without any headaches.

First, you want to research state laws about getting approved for a liquor license. Most states have a specific agency dedicated to controlling and regulating alcoholic beverages. These agencies will provide you all the information you need. For example, in Texas, a liquor license is issued through the Texas Alcohol Beverage Commission (TABC).

The second step is to complete your application from the agency controlling it and to follow their directions. Most of the time handling of a liquor license is done on a local level. Your application will give you information on where to submit. When you submit you can make your fee payments; often one to the state and one to the county. The third step is to make sure you comply with both state and county requirements. Depending on the type of liquor license you are applying for you may need to do an interview, site visit with an inspector, and even a court hearing.

The fourth and final step is to maintain your license by following state laws. Make sure you renew your license within the appropriate time frame in order to avoid delays and potentially lose your license. It is also important you stay up to date on current changes in laws or regulations that can affect your liquor license.

LIQUOR LICENSE CHECKLIST

While each state has slight variations in the requirements for a liquor license, most have similar things you'll need to provide. Let's look at a checklist of the key pieces of personal information you're likely to need when applying for a liquor license so you can be prepared when applying for your liquor license.

The first item on most liquor license checklists is a criminal background check. Most of the time this entails sending in your fingerprints to confirm your identity.

The second thing you'll likely need is a copy of all financial documents. Some states will require at least a year's work of business's sales tax license and real estate tax receipts (But only if you have been in business for a year or more). You'll also likely need a copy of your voter's registration card. Nowadays, most states are also requiring to see either your US birth certificate or Green card if you are an immigrant.

Third, you'll want a photograph of yourself for identity purposes in your liquor license application. The same goes for any business partners you may have. You may also be required to provide a recent photograph of your establishment.

Not all states require a diagram of the floor plan, but quite a few do. If your state requires it, you'll need a floor diagram that includes the length and width of walls, evidence of where all entrances and exits are, exterior areas and a separate diagram of any other floors on the premises.

Most states also require a certificate of good standing. This typically has to be dated within the last 90 days.

Lastly, you want to have your license fee on hand. When applying for a liquor license you typically need to include a check or money order for the license fee. The amount will vary depending on the state you are in and whether there is a city or state fee or both.

INSURANCE

COMMERCIAL INSURANCE

Getting commercial insurance for a bar/nightclub isn't something most owners are comfortable with. As with all types of insurance, this is complicated, and policies are often written in a confusing language that makes it difficult to understand. It can be even harder to compare policies and make sure you are getting the right coverage.

What is Commercial Insurance?

Just what is commercial insurance and what makes it different from other insurance policies? Commercial insurance is similar to the insurance you have on your home. It protects you from property damage and specific activities within your establishment. For example, theft insurance often has to be purchased separately. You should specifically ask what is and isn't covered in the policy to make sure you can get proper coverage for everything that happens in your establishment.

Factors Influencing Cost of Insurance

When it comes to commercial insurance, there are a few factors that have a major impact on the policy rates. Sometimes just a minor change to the way you run your establishment will have a big impact on your insurance policy. Consider the following when getting your commercial insurance.

First, look at how much it will cost to replace everything you own. This is important to know the size of your insurance policy. This should be the cost of the building, the furniture, and all the fixtures. Basically you want to know the cost to rebuild everything and start over again. Within your policy, you need to be aware of the difference between actual cash value and replacement cost. Actual cash value means the cost of everything at the time the incident occurred to destroy them. This value includes depreciation due to wear and tear. On the other hand, replacement cost is the cost that actually occurs to restore everything. You need to consider this when determining the value of your insurance policy.

Another thing to consider is your employees. If you do have employees, you'll need workers compensation insurance in case someone is injured. However, you need to be aware of the fact that if you don't have worker's compensation or liability insurance it can affect you if you need to have construction or redesign work done. Some companies won't work on your properties if your insurance doesn't cover workers while on your premises.

Another thing to consider is whether or not you'll be serving food. The percentage of food you serve to the level of alcoholic beverages will have a big impact on the cost of your commercial insurance. If more than half your sales are in alcohol, then you have a higher liability risk, and your insurance rates are higher. If over half your sales are in food, then a lower cost restaurant insurance policy may be a better option.

Another factor to consider is whether you are going to have live entertainment. If you plan to have special equipment for entertainment, then your rates might increase.

Lastly, you need to be aware of potential natural disasters in your area. In most states disaster insurance for a bar/nightclub is separate. Still, it is always a good idea to be clear on exactly what is and isn't covered.

LIQUOR LIABILITY INSURANCE

It may seem obvious that as an owner of a drinking establishment you need to have liquor liability insurance, yet only about one in three bars/nightclubs actually have this coverage. This coverage is important since it can save you from the kind of legal problems that can close an average establishment without the same protections.

There are a few reasons why one might not include this in their establishment purchase. For most the reason is because they falsely assume that the insurance is included in their main insurance policy. However, the truth is that most commercial insurance policies for bars/nightclubs exclude coverage found in liquor liability insurance. Let's look closer at this insurance and why you should have it.

What is Liquor Liability Insurance?

This insurance covers legal problems that can occur from patrons legally drinking at your establishment. For example, if two patrons get into a fight and a legal problem arises because one of them claims you are responsible because you allowed them to get drunk, then this insurance would cover you.

The insurance also covers you if a patron leaves your bar and gets involved in a car crash, should you get held responsible for the patron's actions. It also covers cases of alcohol poisoning should it occur.

On the other hand, this insurance doesn't protect against illegal alcohol sales, such as knowingly selling to minors. Some states no longer have this insurance as an option and others require it. It is best to check with your state to make sure you are in compliance before opening your establishment.

If you are going to get this coverage then you need to make sure the following is included in your insurance policy:

First, make sure the policy covers legal defenses. Many bar/nightclub insurance policies exclude defense fees. Therefore, make sure the insurance policy includes legal defense fees.

Second, make sure the policy includes assault and battery. A few policies will try to exclude this. This makes your policy virtually worthless since this is a common feature of many lawsuits with liability claims.

Third, you want to make sure the policy has employee liquor liability requirements. While it may seem unlikely that your employees will be drunk on the job and do something troubling, you still want to make sure employees are covered by your insurance policy.

Lastly, you want to make sure your policy includes mental damages. A lot of policies try to avoid paying out for mental damages. However, with so many lawsuits today you should make sure this is included in your policy.

Even if you have proper coverage in your policy, it doesn't mean you have a free ride when it comes to alcohol. You still want to make sure your staff is trained to recognize drunk individuals, how to keep them off the premises and to make sure people can get home safely. Your security should also be trained to take proactive action when customers start causing trouble.

Talk with your insurance provider since some companies will even offer training programs to help train your staff. By doing these programs, you can even sometimes reduce the cost of your insurance policy. These programs definitely offer benefits for your establishment.

Public Liability Insurance

A part of opening your bar/nightclub is making sure it is properly protected from threats, including a number of legal threats that can come up during operations. Another important insurance you need to consider is public liability insurance. It works along with safe working conditions and maintaining premises to protect your establishment from accidents beyond your control.

What Is Public Liability Insurance?

Public liability insurance protects you from claims made by those who injure themselves on your property. It is different from liquor insurance because it doesn't cover what happens when people leave your property. Also, it doesn't cover damage to the property. Rather it is strictly protection for third parties that are injured. Public liability insurance is not only needed to protect you, but also allows you to deal with third parties. Often businesses such as construction companies and cleaning services won't work on your property unless you have public liability coverage. In addition, in some states, it is required as a part of your bar/nightclub insurance package.

What You Need in Public Liability Insurance

Not all forms of insurance are the same. This is why you need to make sure your public liability insurance fully covers you in the event a third party brings a claim against you. You want to make sure your coverage includes the following:

First, you want to make sure the policy covers full defense fees. Policies range from not covering defense fees to only allow partial coverage. The cost of defending yourself in court is often the largest part of your costs. Make sure your policy covers full legal defense.

Make sure the policy also covers your employees with worker compensation insurance. Your employees are at your establishment more than customers and more likely to be injured. This is why you want to have workers compensation insurance as a part of your public liability insurance, even if it isn't required in your state.

Lastly, you want to make sure your insurance policy includes product liability insurance. Even if you don't make products, this coverage helps if you have a salad bar, serve food or mix drinks. For example, if a customer gets food poisoning; this would be covered under this part of the policy.

Theft Insurance

Theft insurance, as with most employee related insurance such as workers compensation insurance, may seem like unnecessary and expensive additions for a new establishment; but you may find it necessary to carry various worker related insurance policies. Let's take a look at theft insurance.

For bar owners, theft is a common problem. Employees may steal drinks or take bottles from the inventory room. Even small thefts can add up over time, but it is often more of a management problem. This isn't the type of theft that you'll need insurance to handle.

Theft insurance works for larger problems such as looting, burglary or robbery. These larger thefts can't be prevented just by security measures. Although security measures such as security cameras, alarm systems, and vigilance can help to an extent; getting insurance can help as well.

Most commercial insurance policies carry theft insurance as a part of their coverage. However, you need to read carefully since not all policies carry full theft coverage. There are three things your theft insurance needs to cover:

First, it needs to cover employee-related thefts. An insurance policy without this coverage is essentially worthless.

Second, it should include armed robbery coverage. While most policies cover this, some sell it for extra if you are in a dangerous area.

Third, a policy needs to cover looting. You should consider where your establishment is located and decide if you want to pay extra for this coverage.

Disaster Insurance

Disaster insurance may seem unnecessary and too expensive. Also, there is some confusion as to why disaster insurance is different from commercial insurance that your bar/nightclub already has. Let's look at what disaster insurance is and why you should consider getting it for your establishment.

Commercial Insurance versus Disaster Insurance

Disaster insurance basically covers any property damage that isn't covered by your regular insurance. For example, commercial insurance will cover fire damage because of an unknown electrical issues or a car driving through the window; but it won't cover fire as a result of an earthquake or a car tossed into your establishment from a tornado. The latter are incidents that would be covered by disaster insurance. It is also why you should purchase the disaster insurance add-on to your commercial insurance.

Disaster insurance is about more than simply restoring your property. There are more costs involved when recovering from a disaster than just rebuilding. You also have the cost of interruption of business. Insurance policies often don't cover these expenses.

Is Disaster Insurance for You?

Whether you decide to include disaster insurance as a part of your commercial insurance or not takes some thought. There are many things that go into deciding to include the cost of this add-on insurance. If you find you live in a high-risk area such as a coastal zone, you may even find you can't get this type of coverage for your establishment.

Another thing you need to consider is the amount of insurance coverage you'll need. If you feel you can simply cash out and start new somewhere else after a disaster, then you probably won't need this level of insurance. However, if you want to stay where you are, then you'll need to consider the cost of disaster insurance. Often disaster insurance is going to cost you about 1/50 the amount of benefit you expect to receive.

You also have to consider that there are two types of disaster insurance for bars/nightclubs. One type covers specific types of events. For example, hurricane coverage would only protect you against hurricanes and not flood. The other type of coverage will cover all events unless specified in the insurance plan. These plans are often more reliable, but more expensive.

BOP (BUSINESS OWNER'S POLICY)

The last word on insurance is, find an agent that sells commercial insurance, ask them to offer you BOP (Business Owner's Policy), this is the best option for most business owner's as this policy covers everything I just mentioned above and much more but under one roof or one umbrella, so to speak.

HOW TO FIND AN EXISTING BAR TO BUY OR LEASE?

If you are new to bar and tavern business but have enough interest to dig deeper, then the next step for you is to try and find a few businesses for sale and evaluate them the best way possible and see if any of them fit your budget and needs.

Bar business as I mentioned earlier is truly a recession-proof business and still provides a comfortable living for a family. Not to mention the freedom it provides by having and owning your own business.

If you are serious about finding a suitable bar business to buy or lease, there are many ways to find a few that are for sale in your area.

You can try both Online and Offline ways.

5 Offline Ways to Find a Business for Sale

- Through Local business brokers (Some national and some local. Two of the major national brokerage companies are Sunbelt and Nationwide business brokers. Local or statewide)

- Through Local commercial real estate agents

- Through Local newspaper classified

- Through Local or national F&B franchise offerings

- Through Vendors (this works better if you are already in this line of business)

5 ONLINE WAYS TO FIND A BUSINESS FOR SALE

There are some very reputable websites you can go and check for sale listings; then there are also online auction houses that sell restaurants among other businesses.

1. First, check out bizbuysell.com. This site is similar to realtor.com for the home real estate, but in this site, business brokers list their businesses that are for sale.

2. Try searching on NRC.com and Loopnet.com. Both of these are big players when it comes to the online business brokerage. You will find both "business for sale" and "business for lease."

3. Craigslist ads. Yes, you can find them under "business for sale."

4. Search auction houses that sell commercial properties

5. You can also just do a google search by typing "restaurant/bar for sale in Los Angeles, Ca" Just mention your city and state and see what comes up.

But before you contact any of the sellers or brokers, you need to have your game plan set, so you don't sound like you are just browsing the market.

Business brokers are very different than typical home real estate agents. If a broker senses that you are not serious, they may not even disclose some of their prime listings to you. The reason is simple; they don't want to take a buyer who is not serious to a seller who is motivated to sell. This can take away from the broker's credibility in front of the seller. Also, sellers typically only want serious and qualified buyers that are ready to buy.

You will notice that, before a broker discloses any information about a business, they will want you to sign a document called an NDA (Non-Disclosure Agreement). This is required because you are being exposed to some confidential and sensitive financial information about a business. Once you sign the NDA, you are in a contract that says you are not to disclose the information you are about to receive with just anyone.

Also, another thing to keep in mind when visiting any of the potential stores for sale, that most times the business owners do not want the employees to know that they are selling the business. Sometimes there is a good reason for it. So first sit down and figure out what your budget is, what your game plan is, and how soon you want to get into a business. Once you know these three, you are halfway there.

Just remember when you contact a business broker, they may ask you a lot of questions to figure out what, exactly, you are looking for. They may ask about your budget; it is usually a good idea not to answer that with a dollar figure, instead tell them that it varies depending on what is out there. This way they will show you a wide range of businesses. Some may be over your budget, and some below, but this way you can see where the market stands. It gives you a baseline of the highs and the lows of your market.

Once you have a list of 3-4 businesses to look at that is when your real work starts. First, you need to visit all the locations, so you have a visual feel for them. Take plenty of notes. A good way is to take notes where you write down the good / bad on each side so later you can see what the good points are and what the bad points are of a business and if the bad ones outweigh the good ones.

You can also use a marketing tool I often use called an MA-CP grid, where you draw a square box with 4 mini squares that are equal to the square in that big box and, on the left of this box, I write MA, which stands for market attractiveness and on the bottom I write CP or competitive positioning. I try to place each of the bars in one of those squares based on their location, sales, nearest competitors, etc.

If a bar has very high market attractiveness, you should place it on the high side of the quadrant. Similarly, if another one has a very good competitive position in the market, it should be placed on the "high" side as well. Ideally, you want to pick the store/business that ranks high on both market attractiveness and competitive positioning. This way you know you are looking at a winner.

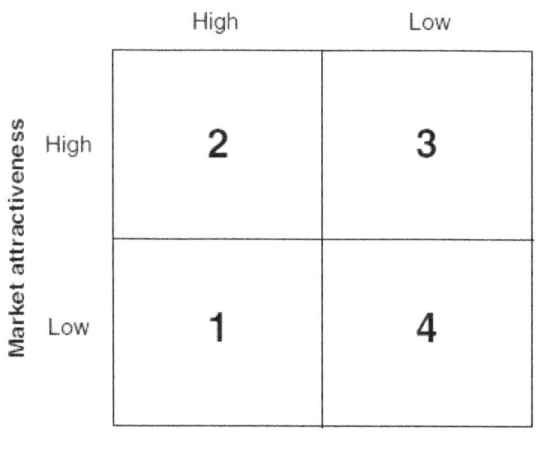

Once you narrow down to, let's say, 1-2 bars out the 5, time to tell your broker or seller that you are interested in finding out more about their business.

If you have come this far, then you are well on your way to be a business owner. But before you say yes, remember, once you narrow down to handful of bars, it is time to do due diligence on each of your findings.

Once you do good and thorough work, the right one will come out of that bunch, and you will know which business is the right one for you to make an offer on.

FINDING A SUITABLE LOCATION

Yes, finding a great location is essential to your business's success. A question may come to your mind, what is so important about your business location?

Well, let's see, your business place /location is one of the most critical parts of your survival because location can make or break a business. You may have the best cocktails, food, and service but if the facility is not clean, not inviting, not well lit, does not have easy in and out access, then the chances are that business will fail or not succeed to its fullest potential.

The reality is when choosing what location you need to lease, first and foremost your attention should be at the facility itself or place and its layout and access, remember there are a few things you can change and improve, and there are some things you can not. For example, if the in and out access to the facility is difficult, you can not change that. On the other hand, if the facility is not well lit or dirty and unclean, you can most likely change that with minimal effort.

When doing the location research, try to come up with a handful of sites, write them all down then analyze each and every one of them based on their advantages and disadvantages. See which one comes to the top based on your research.

Location -1	Advantage	Disadvantage

Location -2	Advantage	Disadvantage

Once you fill the blocks in with all the advantage points and disadvantage points for each location, you will see which scores the highest with most advantage points.

Alternatively, you can also use a SWOT Analysis tool like this below. It is very self-explanatory, take a look.

SWOT ANALYSIS

Strengths (internal, positive factors) Strengths describe the positive attributes, tangible and intangible, of your organization. These are within your control.	**Weaknesses** (internal, negative factors) Weaknesses are aspects of your business that detract from the value you offer or place you at a competitive disadvantage

Opportunities (external, positive factors) Opportunities are external attractive factors that represent reasons for your business to exist and prosper	**Threats** (external, negative factors) Threats are external factors beyond your control that could put your business at risk. You may benefit from having contingency plans for them.

Once you know the ideal location, time to start negotiating your lease. A commercial lease is very different than most residential leases. Most commercial leases are often quoted as per-square-feet in dollar amount which typically doesn't include CAM (Common Area Maintenance). You have to add both costs then multiply that number with your exact leased square footage to know what you will be paying.

Did you know that a commercial lease can have a clause where the landlord can get you out of business in just 30 days? How about the other clause where they can walk-in to your premises even when you are closed, and no one is at your location? It is always a good idea to have your lease reviewed by an attorney, so you know what is in that lease.

It is also a good idea to negotiate an exit strategy at least for the first year, so in the event your business doesn't flourish as you imagine, you can get out within the first year without having to pay any more penalties or other fees.

Seven Most Important Factors to Consider When Leasing a Facility

Demographic

It is important to consider foot traffic during the process of picking a location for your new bar. However, keep in mind you can have a large amount of foot traffic around or behind the store where they are not actually seeing you or passing your store. Foot traffic is only helpful when you establish yourself as the neighborhood hangout joint.

To know whether or not this foot traffic will be in your target market is such an important step when you open a bar and it can have a considerable influence on your location choice. Think about where this foot traffic is coming from.

No matter how great the location seems, the better choice would be to open your bar near other businesses or an office park. Remember that when you choose your location, it will always affect your profitability either adversely or positively based on how smart you are when picking the location, your goal is always to make choices that will impact your profitability positively.

As I mentioned earlier, doing a thorough analysis of each proposed location is vital. It is not only essential, but it is beneficial to think about more out of the box competitors. These would be anyplace that would allow your targeted customers to get what you provide.

Look at places such as Bar and Grill type restaurants, or even casual diners that sell cocktails, beer, and wine. These businesses are in different markets; they are all basically competing with the products you have.

Think about what other businesses are around your bar; sometimes some of these companies can help you by actually complementing your offerings. Having your bar near other businesses or a college could encourage students and employees to come to you first because of the added convenience of your location.

If you are near a mall or shopping center, you could receive traffic from those looking for a cold one, while walking around and shopping.

ACCESSIBILITY

While customers will come back if the quality of your product offerings is good, if you are convenient, they are more likely to give you a try. Think about what your customer needs.

If they're driving cars, you have to provide convenient parking. For customers walking to or from various other locations, it is critical to be clearly visible from the street, without street accessibility, you could lose your customers to your competitors.

BUILDING INFRASTRUCTURE

Many times bars need a specific kind of building infrastructure. It is important to understand that not all spaces will be able to accommodate an F&B retail outlet. In most situations, you are looking for a cozy and comfortable space that fits the average number of customers you plan on having without feeling too crowded.

You also need to remember to make sure that the place has adequate plumbing, electrical, and other utilities that are required to establish a bar.

Another thing to consider besides the actual space is licensure. Some spaces don't allow certain liquor permits on their property. Make sure that you have inquired about this when you are choosing venues for your bar. You might want to check with your local city or county business licensing office to see if there are any such restrictions.

TERMS OF THE LEASE

When thinking of all the questions you will have to consider, the most obvious question that is often thought about when you are looking for the right location is "Can I afford it?" and "Can my customers afford it?"

If you choose a location with high rent costs, remember those costs will have to be transferred to your customers in the form of cocktail or beer prices. While that isn't necessarily a bad thing, you have to keep the targeted customer in mind while making sure your prices are in line with your competitors.

You also need to think about whether a location needs any renovations. Small business loans are used to help cover building costs, so make sure you factor that into your loan.

After the cost of your building, there are a few lease terms you to be aware of that would help you figure out the best location for your shop. Here are some examples of these:

LENGTH OF THE LEASE

Remember that commercial leases are legally binding contracts. You are generally unable to easily break or change any of the terms. Talk to a lawyer, and get a full understanding before signing any agreements.

Read your lease and make sure you know if the landlord will be allowed to increase your rent after the lease is signed. Also, know the insurance requirements. Different leases can require you to have a specific kind of insurance coverages that could increase your overall budget.

SECURITY DEPOSIT

Make sure that you know the conditions for your security deposit return. It is essential to understand how much you will have to pay upfront and the exact process of getting that security deposit back. It is important to know who is responsible for maintaining the space and who is responsible for the costs.

NEGOTIATING THE BAR BUSINESS LEASE

You have to know what you want. In lease negotiation, your goal is to create a situation where everyone leaves feeling as if they have won. It is your responsibility to know what you want and consistently pursue it.

Your potential landlord is looking out for their best interest, and you should be looking out for yours as well. If something is important to you, make sure to have it in writing. A verbal agreement won't be enough.

Your lease can be very limiting if you allow it to be. Make sure that what want is actually located somewhere in the language of your lease. Rank what you want in three steps:

1. Must Haves
2. Negotiable
3. Reaches

Remember that if you don't ask for it, you absolutely won't get it.

Understand what your potential landlord wants. Listen to what their goals entail, and then modify your negotiations to meet their needs as well. Make sure to listen to what they are giving in to, and what they are fighting for. Remember that absolutely everything is negotiable, but show some discretion and restraint when considering what to negotiate, whether it be services rendered or money.

Sometimes the rent just can't be changed, but CAM, construction cost and other building costs might be able to be negotiated.

Strive to find your best middle ground. Negotiating is all give and take. State what you want, and the reasons you want it.

Then tell them why it is essential to your business's success and then listen to their point of view as well. Then give up what you really don't need, for what they feel is very important.

PLANNING & BUILD-OUT

PLANNING STAGE

As I mentioned earlier, depending on your city, county and state's requirements, and the location you are trying to lease, you may be required to submit some type of plans of what you are trying to accomplish.

It could be as little as a simple hand-drawn plan for your local county health state liquor licensing department showing what and how you will lay out your bar, seating and serving areas. If you are planning on installing a certain type of cooking equipment such as a commercial fryer or a grill, then you may be required to install a commercial ventilation hood system. So be aware of that as it can get very expensive very fast.

If you are planning on offering fried food (remember the fried mozzarella sticks I was talking about earlier) then yes, you will need a commercial fryer. Depending on your city and county fire code, they may require you to install a vent-hood system for your fryers. Most natural gas-powered fryers and even ovens do require some type of ventilation systems, so check with your local fire dept.

In the event, if you need a total makeover, meaning you are asked to rebuild a whole interior of a building (total build-out), you will need to hire an architect to get a set of plans drawn. But for this to happen, you will need to furnish specific information to your architect.

1. How many seats you want in the facility
2. A list of all equipment you will be using along with their specs so an electrical design can be drawn based on the actual load.
3. How many restrooms you will need
4. What type of lighting fixtures you prefer to install
5. If you will need any walk-in cooler or freezer in the facility
6. All plumbing requirements according to the health department code (if you will need a three compartment sink, a mop sink, etc.)
7. A layout of your counters and checkout stand

8. The exact area of placement for all your reach-in coolers

Once you provide such information, the architect will then start drawing up the all the plans along with an HVAC plan based on the current city or county code.

Once they are done with the plan, they will send it off to your city or county building inspector for proper approval. Once the set of plans are approved, then your work will start.

Time for you to either hire a general contractor or if it is allowed in your city, you can act as the general contractor and hire sub-contractors to finish various jobs that need to be done according to the plan.

For example, you can hire a licensed plumber to do all the plumbing work, hire an HVAC company to get all your AC related work done and so on.

Last time I had to get a full set of plans for a franchise fast food restaurant, it cost me around $8,500, but that was a full set of plans which included everything from wall décor to HVAC and everything in between.

Before you get nervous, let me assure you, if you are just opening a bar, chances are you won't have to do all that. But I wanted to mention this because in certain cities or states all these may be requirements based on what you are renting.

It may not be a bad idea to discuss your goal and plans with the city or county health board to get an idea of what might be involved, this way you will be better prepared for what will come next.

BUILD-OUT

This is a stage where you see your bar comes to life little by little. Whatever you envisioned it to be, you will now see it coming together piece by piece.

Regardless if you hired a general contractor or an interior designer, this is the stage where things will happen fast. So make sure to have all your ducks in a row.

Make sure to install/place all your big equipment before installing the counter tops, this way you won't have any gaps or holes. Get any and all HVAC, plumbing and electrical work done.

Test out all your electrical components to make sure everything is in working condition. Once that is done, time to start painting the walls. Hang all the decors once you are done painting.

But before you bring in furniture, lay your floor tiles or wood planks, whichever you picked. Let the floor settle for a few days before bringing in the furniture.

Once you are done with all this, time to call on your health and building inspector for their final inspection so you can get the CO (certificate of occupancy) without which you cannot open your business.

SIGNAGE & MENU

While a bar sign isn't likely to make or break your business, they do serve a number of purposes and can help with your establishment's overall image. Let's first look at the uses for a sign for your establishment to build your image, increase business and help efficiency.

First and foremost a sign helps with building an establishment's identity. A neon sign will give a different impression from a vintage sign. Also, a sign with a mirror will help provide a greater sense of space.

Using a sign can be helpful to draw in patrons if your entrance is difficult to spot. An open sign is also helpful to let people know that you are actually open since at night things can easily look dark and closed.

While some states require signs for safety, this is a good idea even if it isn't required. Signs are indicating where exits and fire extinguishers are mandatory by your local fire code for safety. In addition, lighted signs advertising the brands of alcohol you have on hand and also help light areas that might be little dark.

Lastly, signs can be a great way to promote your new drinks and/or specials. Some people notice visual things better than hearing. So having a way for people to see what you are offering rather than just relying on wait staff to tell them is a good way to increase your sales. It can also be good if you have a noisy bar where it can be difficult to communicate with patrons.

Here is a place where I had one of my menus designed, the site is www.99designs.com

The best thing about this place, you can have many designers bid on your project and show you a mockup design, you pick the best looking one and pay only one designer not 20 of them. The cost is less than $500.

You should also have a logo for your bar. You can get the logo design done at 99designs.com or if you have limited budget try fiverr.com. This is a place where you can find talents from all around the world ready to take any task for $5 only. This is my go-to site for many jobs like simple logo designs to social media marketing.

Once you have your logo, make sure to order business cards, bags, boxes and other packaging accessories for your bar. You can get a local printing press to do this job or find many online printing services that can do the same job for much cheaper.

DÉCOR & FURNITURE

When planning your establishment, you need to think about the furniture you're going to need. Have a checklist and use this to generate ideas for the types of furniture that will work well with your theme and style. Let's look at the essential furniture you're going to need.

FIXED FURNITURE

If you bought an existing establishment then you likely already have some furniture. Or you may have a completely empty space, and you need to determine where your fixed furniture will be. These items need to be considered first since they will determine the layout for your establishment.

Obviously the most important part of your establishment is the bar. This doesn't have to be the huge mahogany and brass bar you remember seeing. No matter what type of bar you choose to install, the most important thing to consider is placement since this will influence nearly every other aspect of your establishment. The most common placement is often at the center of the establishment. This makes it easier for patrons to get a drink.

Another piece of built-in furniture to consider is booths. While this may not be an efficient use of space for some, it can help anchor the layout of a room, and some patrons prefer a more private space to spend their time. Just make sure you don't overdo it with booths since they can place too much constraint on your establishment.

STOOLS

This is a common feature in many bar/nightclub settings. There are a few things you need to know about stools before choosing them for your establishment.

The first thing you need to know is that stools come in both a fixed and movable form. Fixed stools are typically used around the bar and tend to be sturdier. However, since they can't be moved there will be some constraints involved. Movable stools come in three sizes and can be used both at the bar and around activities such as pool tables.

MOBILE FURNITURE

A major mobile furniture you'll need to consider is tables. While these can be fixed, it is best to choose movable options since it gives you greater flexibility in your layout. You can choose the standard dining table or a high pub table.

OUTDOOR FURNITURE

You may not need to worry about this unless you have a separate outdoor space at your establishment. If you do need outdoor furniture, it is pretty much the same as the indoor furniture but needs to be durable enough to withstand the elements. They should also be easy to clean and store at the end of the day.

Sound and Lighting

One important aspect of planning your bar/nightclub is the lighting. No matter what style of bar/nightclub you are planning to open, you want to make sure the lighting is perfect. Consider some important areas of your establishment that need specific lighting styles and techniques.

Booths and Other Intimate Areas

If you have an intimate area such as a booth, then you should use soft lighting. Try warm orange colors or the illusion of flickering candles. You can also consider lounge lights with glass wall accents to give a romantic half-light; this is an especially good option if your establishment is decked out with dark wood finishes.

Dance Floors and Other Focal Points

For focal points, you want flashy and modern lighting. The best solution for this is LED lighting. Use LED lights for bar shelves, bottle displays, and dance floors, dining and drinking areas.

CONTROLLED LIGHTING

Perhaps the most important thing is to be able to control your lighting. This can be helpful for promotional nights when you need to change your atmosphere for the right customer.

You'll also want control over dimming your lights. This allows you to turn up the lights at the closing time to signal everyone to leave or to change the mood depending on the atmosphere.

SPILLOVER AND HARSH TRANSITIONS

There are two practical considerations to make when planning your establishment's lighting. First is spillover lighting. Certain areas of your establishment need to be well lit so people can function properly such as the kitchen, bathroom, and storage areas. However, you don't want these areas near a darker intimate area since the harsh spillover of the lights can ruin the mood. Second, you want to have well placed transitional lighting in areas such as hallways going outside or to the bathrooms, so people aren't affected by the sudden change in light when coming or going from your establishment or certain areas.

STAGE LIGHTING

Perhaps one of the most important lighting areas for your establishment is the stage if you are going to have one in your place. While the lighting will vary slightly depending on the act, there are some basic elements you want to consider.

ILLUMINATION LEVELS

The first thing to consider is your level of illumination or how bright you want to make the performers. This has to do with visibility. If you have a single person on the stage, then the lighting goal is simple, highlight the facial expressions of the person. However, if you have a large band, then you may need different levels of brightness at different points in the show and focused on different people.

COLOR EFFECTS

While the color of lighting is more subtle, it is still important for setting the right mood. Soft blue light works well for jazz type music, and a rock band is going to need more red coloring. All of the colors will help raise the mood and feeling of the music.

LIGHTING ANGLES

The right mix of stage and lighting comes through proper lighting angles. If you need to light a single person, you will need two spots pointing at the person at forty-five degrees.

SPECIAL EFFECTS

For bands, you may also need to consider some special effects. Dimmers can allow you to fade stage lights between songs or sets. For dance clubs, you'll need things like lasers, eliminators, and foggers to help set the right mood.

SUPPLIES AND EQUIPMENT

Once you have the necessary permits and financing to start a bar/nightclub, then it is time to gather the right equipment for your establishment. You need to make sure your establishment is fully equipped to not only meet the needs of your patrons but your staff as well.

A well-stocked establishment needs to have all the essentials. The first thing you need to source is glassware. You need a wide variety of glasses that work for the types of drinks your establishment offers. You'll also need a number of spare glasses on hand since accidental breakage happens both from customers and staff alike.

Likewise, you want to purchase glassware that is durable and meets safety standards.

There are also other equipment needs you will want to consider. If you have a trendy bar offering cocktails and mixed drinks you'll need a rail behind the bar offering mixers, pourers, shakers, strainers and glass rimmers, so you have them when you need them.

Other items you may find essential include bottle openers, corkscrews, ice buckets, countertop mats and other essentials.

It is essentialt to have equipment that helps with maintaining health and hygiene of your establishment. You'll need the proper cleaning products on hand. Plus for good, clean glassware you'll want dependable dishwashing hardware.

Hardware is important for a bar/nightclub owner. Some things you'll need include wine coolers, refrigeration units, beer dispensers, traps, sinks and ice makers. You'll also need a cash register to process payments. We'll discuss more of these items in detail later so you can make the right decisions.

Buying or Leasing Equipment

A lot of cost goes into starting a bar/nightclub. There is the down payment, liquor license, advertising, hiring and on top of all this, you'll still need to equip the bar/nightclub. In fact, equipment is one of the biggest expenses when starting your establishment.

Some think a solution is to buy used equipment. However, when you buy used equipment, you are faced with the cost of maintaining it and still having to replace it at some point. In addition, broken equipment can lead to a negative experience for staff and customers. Rather, a solution you can consider is leasing your equipment. Let's look at the benefits.

Leasing Benefits

There are four benefits to leasing equipment for your establishment.

First, if your equipment breaks, you don't have to pay costs for repairs. Rather you just return it and get a new one.

Second, leasing reduces your startup costs. New equipment can easily cost you thousands of dollars. You pay a fraction of this when leasing.

Third, once the lease ends you can often renew the lease and move up to a new model. Leasing means you don't have to worry about old equipment breaking down when you use it.

Fourth, Leasing gives you better tax breaks since it is a recurring fee every year.

One important fact I need to mention is that leasing is only beneficial for large expensive equipment but don't try to lease mixing blenders are anything that small.

Here are some online websites you can visit and compare good quality new and used furniture and equipment. You can also search for a few local used equipment dealers this way you get to see everything first hand and best of all there is no shipping cost.

https://www.acitydiscount.com/Bar-Equipment.1.25362.2.1.htm

http://www.allthebestequipment.com/products.php?cat=74

http://www.ebay.com/bhp/used-restaurant-equipment

MANAGEMENT AND EMPLOYEES

This is a vast topic and a crucial one. You can have the best location, best-tasting cocktails, best snacks, and low prices but without the right people behind the bar, you won't be able to see success. The right staffing is one of the fundamental keys to your success.

10 STEP PROCESS ON HOW TO HIRE, TRAIN AND RETAIN EMPLOYEES.

- Where and how to find the right people to hire?

- Asking the right question during an interview
- Providing proper training
- Employee appearance
- Motivating and empowering your employees
- Teaching them marketing 101
- Rewarding the right behavior
- How to discipline bad behavior
- Setting up target & goal oriented incentives
- Regular employee meetings and coaching

There will most likely be a point where you need to take on staff to help you run your business. If this is your first time, it can seem like a complicated and difficult process. Beyond the actual recruitment, you will need to have comprehensive training as well as management strategies already in place. There also needs to be a disciplinary process in case you encounter issues. There are many benefits of having a bar business staff.

An important one is being able to reduce your own workload. It would mean that you would have more time to concentrate on other areas of the shop. However, there are also a few downfalls that come with having employees. You could end up not hiring the right people. You also have to entrust the fate of your business to a total stranger.

It is important to know your exact staffing need.

Consider what your competitors are doing. Look at any other bars nearby that are roughly similar in size to yours. See if they have staff members, and how many are working on any given shift. You might want to consider if you are neglecting other aspects of the business, like prepping and preparation before opening and after closing the shop.

Finally consider if you are experiencing a seasonal rush, is it during the winter holiday months? You might be getting considerably more business because people are out shopping when it's cold outside. If your current state is due to something temporary, consider hiring seasonal employees to get you through your busy stretch.

If you have decided that your bar could benefit from taking on staff, the next step you have to take is to advertise. Before doing this, it's important to consider the type of person that would be well suited to fulfill your shop's needs.

For kitchen and waiting staff your hire should be a people person. They should have a happy, bubbly personalities so they can deliver a friendly, personable service to customers.

While experience is helpful to have, a sweet, and charming nature can be much more appealing to an employer. You can always train someone to make the best cocktails or fried mushrooms, but you can't teach someone to be more personable than they are.

For kitchen staff you will probably want to hire people that have experience. This means that you should be looking for someone who has already worked in a professional kitchen and can cope with pressure-filled situations.

When you write your job listing, make sure that you list any personality requirements or other things that you feel are appropriate. Make sure to set the standard high in order to get what your bar needs.

Once you have hired the best employees, you might need to do some training. If this is the case, then you may want to create a training plan to make sure that all topics are covered. Many shop owners hire staff on a trial basis.

This is so that you can see their suitability. Make sure that you have defined specific goals that you want the employees to achieve by the end of the probationary period. This will enable you to measure their progress. You also might want the new staff members to start on slower days.

For the more experienced new employees you could throw them in at the deep end during your busiest days, and they should do well.

No matter how well you hire, there is always a chance that you would have to deal with poor performance or general misconduct of staff members. It is helpful to have a written disciplinary procedure to follow. Ensure that you have made your staff aware of this procedure when you hire them.

There are a variety of problems that could happen. Performance issues can include poor customer service, repeated failure to meet set goals or simply an unwillingness to carry out responsibilities. Also, conduct-related issues can typically include negligence or poor attendance.

I typically let all new hires know that every new hire is on mandatory probation for 60 days, as that is the evaluation period. I also let them know that during this 60 days, they can be terminated without any prior notice. For example, Georgia is an employer-at-will state, meaning in that state you can fire anyone at any time without reason.

But wait before you get excited, let me also mention that this law does not save you from paying unemployment claims. But it does save you from getting sued if there is not foul play, such as discrimination, involved. So check with your state law to know what and how your state's employment law works.

As the owner and manager, you have the responsibility to address any type of issue with your employees. Then discover the cause of the problem and present a potential resolution with them. It could be the case that you need to remove a member of staff from your shop. This depends on the severity of the actions.

This is an unfortunate scenario, but if it does arise, there are some considerations that you should make first. You should consider if this is the first offense. You need to consider if you have given the employee a fair warning about this issue.

Discover if there are any potential legal implications that could relate to the firing of the employee. On the flip side of that, you need to find a suitable replacement, or you could be stuck filling in shifts until you can hire someone.

Customer service and engagement are always a place for improvements. There's always something that you can do to make your bar business more welcoming to your customers.

For many bar businesses, merely perfecting the most basic of techniques such as remembering the names of regulars and having a smiling staff can provide a significant boost to business prosperity. The following tips will help you to keep the most important aspect of your company happy and functioning correctly.

As I previously stated customers are one of the most important factors in your bar business's success, without them, you don't have a business. It is important to make the goal of adopting a customer-centric focus across the entire staff.

It can help to encourage return customers, build your bar's reputation and grow your overall customer base. A high level of customer service can also be an important difference between you and the other competitors

When you're caught up in the rush of a busy day at the bar, it's easy to accidentally stop smiling and focus only on churning through as many customers as possible. You don't want your staff to forget to add a personal touch to their service.

We as humans are social creatures. A little bit of interaction can go a very long way. There are a variety of ways to help customers feel valued. Greeting customers as they enter helps to create a warm experience for each customer.

Eye contact is so important; make eye contact as you're serving them. And doing this while engaging in small talk and chit chat is one of the best things you can do for your customer experience. Also, anticipating the needs of customers, and providing those needs can make everyone feel comfortable.

Time frames are another factor; be honest about how long the order will take and be apologetic when that time frame takes too long.

Most businesses have their own regular customers, and the same is likely to be true for you. Remember, a regular comes in many types. It could be someone who comes in every day on their way to work or school, or someone who comes for a special treat a few times a month.

It's so essential that you make the time to identify and take note of these people, then make an effort to really get to know them. Regular customers have a noticeable influence on your word of mouth advertising. They are often a lifeline for your business during slow periods where you may not have many other customers.

Once you get to know your regulars, take the time to make sure that they absolutely know they're appreciated. Simple things, such as giving away a free drink every so often, can go a long way in keeping their loyalty.

Make sure you are always taking customer complaints seriously. Dealing with unhappy customers is not ever easy. There are certain things you can do to handle complaints calmly. The most important thing to do is to actually listen to what the customer is saying.

Getting feelings of empathy and understanding from you will make them much more likely to come to a satisfactory resolution with you.

While the adage "The customer is always right" exists, it is not necessarily true. However, it is important that you figure out when to give in, and when it is best to stand your ground.

There are many resolutions to every problem. Whatever the cost may be of giving a customer a free coffee, isn't nearly as much as losing a customer completely.

In other situations, the problem may be best solved by sitting down with the customer and trying to mutually understand each other's perspective so that you both can come to a mutually beneficial resolution.

HIRING

As the owner of a bar/nightclub, one skill you will need to perfect is hiring. When you post an open job position, you will be flooded with applicants, and your job is to find the right qualified candidates for the right positions. This process involves interviewing and hiring the right employees. Let's take a look at how you can streamline this hiring process and how you can find the ideal employee for your establishment.

SORTING APPLICATIONS

The first step you need to take is to sort out the many applications you receive. It is best to sort these into three groups:
1. Near Perfect Applications
2. Okay Applications
3. Problem Applications

As long as you have five or more in the first two piles, you can simply throw out all the applications in the third pile. Although you may want to hold onto them at least until interviews are finished.

THE INTERVIEW PROCESS

No matter what position you are hiring, you want to make sure you schedule a face to face interview. This is the second step in the hiring process.

Any jobs in the hospitality industry rely on first impressions. Therefore, pay attention to first impressions when someone comes in for an interview. Do they seem like a good fit for your establishment? Keep in mind that the person you hire is going to represent your establishment. People need to make a good impression in an interview, and if they don't, then you can just imagine what they would be like with customers.

If you have time, you should look over the resume carefully and find the right questions to ask. Be sure to ask questions that aren't very easy such as:

- How do you handle customers who drink too much?
- What do you do if you suspect a wait staff is pocketing another's tips?
- Why did you leave your last job?
- What are your weaknesses?

The answers are important, but you also want to pay attention to how a person handles the questions. If someone needs you to repeat the question or replies softly, then they may not be the best at communicating in a noisy bar/nightclub.

The best employees are those who are social and in tune with others. They should be high in energy with a positive attitude that makes them confident and comfortable around others. These are important qualities when considering employees to hire for your establishment.

If a potential employee doesn't have a background in a pub/nightclub, then you should look for other qualities that would make them a good fit for your establishment. Those with the social skills needed to succeed in the bar/nightclub scene.

WORKING INTERVIEW

If you are trying to hire to fill a critical position, such as a bartender; then the best way to get a feel for them is to do a working interview. If you haven't opened yet, at least have them mix a drink or serve a table. Not only pay attention to how they do it, but also how comfortable they seem to be. If you still aren't sure, you can always hire them for a week trial to see how they do. However, always remember to never expect perfection.

SCHEDULING

Managing and owning a bar/nightclub also means you need to properly schedule your employees in addition to managing your inventory. Whether you hire someone or do it yourself; a manager needs to direct, control and plan all activities in a bar/nightclub. A strong manager is one who is healthy and happy while also being collaborative, creative, innovative, accountable and decisive.

A manager needs to use planning, supervising and allocating in order to schedule strong employees to take on the day-to-day operations of a bar/nightclub. Proper work scheduling is also important to empower employees by delegating duties and furthering their experience. Empowering your employees will help contribute towards making them strong employees. Consider the following when scheduling your employees.

SCHEDULING ACCORDING TO CHANGES IN CUSTOMER DEMAND

An important part of managing is to schedule your wait staff according to the level of customer demand since this has a direct impact on the customers. As a manager, you need to be aware of the daily flow of customers so you can adjust the number of staff for each shift based on the surge or decline in customers.

SCHEDULING FOR INVENTORY CONTROL

A manager also needs to make sure the inventory of a bar/nightclub is well managed. You can do this by allocating the inventory management duty to a storekeeper. You can also choose to allocate the tracking of the sales to the bartender. This allows you to monitor the inventory and the sales you make. However, when scheduling these tasks make sure you have adequate staff covering all shifts.

RESCHEDULING TO COVER ABSENT EMPLOYEES

There is always going to be times when employees are absent such as off-days, sickness, maternity leave, suspension and other factors that you have no control over as manager. For brief periods you don't need to hire temporary replacement staff unless two or more staff are going to be absent since this loss can impact the collaboration and creativity of strong employees. Often the best option to deal with temporary absent employees is to reschedule duties so that the current employees can fill in for the absent employees.

SCHEDULING CLEANING AND MAINTENANCE TASKS

A manager also needs to make sure the bar/nightclub is cleaned and maintained on a regular basis. Cleanliness is paramount in the bar/nightclub business. Therefore, you need to schedule employees to clean floors, furniture, glasses and other utensils regularly. The best way to accomplish this is through multi-tasking and ensuring all employees take turns in cleaning and maintenance duties.

ONLINE EMPLOYEE TRAINING SITES

For online employee training here are few sites that have shown great results.

http://be-happy4you-in-cyprus.blogspot.com/2013/03/bar-staff-training-manual.html

http://www.businessplanhut.com/employee-training-guide-bartender

https://restauranttrainingmanuals.com/shop/?gclid=Cj0KCQjw1q3VBRCFARIsAPHJXrHSQZodl45VxoK5uYLiHcr3wTXPXq-Jjn9fOwLVc-UTeBfyY5um7MgaArAYEALw_wcB

http://www.five-startraining.com/restaurant_manuals_Bartender.html

FINDING SUPPLIERS AND VENDORS

Bars/nightclubs have very low margins and as a result, need to find a good supplier and vendor to keep costs down while having a quality product. Having the right supplies makes all the difference between a successful establishment and one that fails.

When it comes to vendors and suppliers your first consideration is obviously price. You need to keep costs down, especially when starting a new establishment. However, this shouldn't be your only concern. There is often a reason why a supplier can offer you things at a lower rate than usual. Always make sure you check out the quality of what is being offered since your ultimate goal is customer experience. Let's look at what type of suppliers you need and how to choose the right ones.

First, there are the general bar suppliers; those that give you the basics from toilet paper to straws. There is no shortage of suppliers in this area, but the key is to buy in bulk to save on cost.

Then there are your glassware suppliers. Breakages occur, and you are going to be replacing glassware at some point. You want to choose a glassware supplier that you like working with and establishing a recurring relationship, so you will be able to get replacement glassware at a discount.

Perhaps the bulk of your stock is going to come from alcohol vendors. Depending on the drinks your establishment offers you may have one or more vendors. If you offer beer on tap, consider going with distributors that offer to clean the taps each delivery to help you save time and money. You may also want to consider going with local alcohol so you can both benefit each other.

Lastly, you are going to need a supplier of uniforms and linens. You should choose one that also offers to launder for you since this will save you time and expense. Having uniforms may not be a need, but if your establishment is more upscale, then you may need uniforms to be successful and present a good image.

FINDING VENDORS

The job of researching and finding vendors has become a lot easier thanks to the internet. Simply search for bar supplies, and you'll find a number of vendor options. However, you'll still need to do your research and comparison shop. When doing this, there are a few things to consider.

First, you want to compare delivery costs. A lot of vendors will add the delivery cost into the quote they give you while others add a separate delivery charge to your orders.

Second, you want to look for extra services. Sometimes it can be better to go with a more expensive vendor if they provide you with extra services that saves you money in the long run. For example, some beer vendors offer to clean your taps when they deliver. Always look for money-saving add-ons.

Third, is to consider selection. Does the distributor have a style that matches your bar? Does a different vendor offer you a better match?

Lastly, you want to look into the delivery schedule. Make sure they deliver on a day and time that works for you. Also, make sure you have enough storage space for the number of deliveries you receive.

Consider all four of these areas when choosing a supplier and vendor. Remember that staying supplied is key to have a successful establishment. So make sure you establish yourself with a strong supplier/vendor and don't ever take them for granted.

One great way to find specific liquor and wine vendors in your area are to either go through the yellow pages (phone book) or any business directory or look for "wine and liquor wholesalers."

As for finding the beer wholesalers, follow the same search path, and you will be able to locate your local Budweiser and Miller distributors.

HOW TO MANAGE INVENTORY

One of the hardest tasks in the bar industry is taking proper inventory. It's a long process involving late nights for managers and bartenders in the storeroom. Inventory tracking is especially important for bars, where frequent spills and free drinks can hurt your profitability.

While there is bar software that can help with the bar inventory management process, it's best to understand the basics of how this is normally handled with pen-and-paper. Even if you plan on using restaurant inventory software, having a deep understanding of how liquor inventory is done will help you make better purchasing decisions.

Here's a look at how to do liquor and bar inventory for your bar, tavern or club.

BAR INVENTORY BASICS

When looking at bar inventory, maintaining enough on-hand inventory to generate sales is only the beginning. Your bar inventory also helps with determining how your bar is performing financially.

- Measuring shrinkage.
- Setting inventory minimums.
- Identifying beverage costs so you can price effectively.
- Pinpointing which drinks are the best-selling and most profitable in your bar.

Ultimately, your goal is to calculate your inventory usage within a certain period so you can compare it to your sales.

CALCULATING INVENTORY USAGE

To get your bar's inventory usage for a period of time, you'll need to know your inventory at the beginning of the period, how much you have at the end of the period, and how much you received during the period.

Here's the formula to determine your inventory usage:

Usage (Sold) = Starting inventory + Liquor Purchased – Ending Inventory

Simple, right? It's just what you once *had* minus what you now *have*.

Once you know your usage, you can use this information to gather useful data to manage your bar better.

One example of how you can use the above formula is to **estimate your pour cost** – simply divide the result of the above formula by total sales.

$$\frac{\text{Usage (Sold)}}{\text{Total Sales}} = \text{Pour Cost}$$

Knowing your pour cost can help you determine better pricing for your drinks.

You can also use your usage to estimate how much inventory you'll need to purchase in the following periods, and how frequently you'll need to make these inventory purchases. By getting into a regular ordering routine and altering it as your sales change, your bar can be prepared.

Using this formula to determine the usage of individual drinks in your bar will help you run a more cost-effective business.

LIQUOR INVENTORY

Now that you know the formula, it's time to get into how to do liquor inventory.

There's a lot that goes into calculating inventory usage, but a fundamental way to handle it is with a bar inventory spreadsheet.

Your spreadsheet should have these columns:

- Starting inventory
- Received inventory
- Ending inventory
- Alcohol type

You should also include rows for identifying your alcohol, such as:

- Alcohol type
- Brand
- Name
- Bottle size

Here is an example, but you can add more rows as I mentioned above, you can customize it to fit your personal needs.

MONTHLY LIQUOR INVENTORY SPRREADSHEET					
Brand Type	Size	Beg Invtry	Purchase	End Invtry	Sold
Jhonny Walker	1.75 L	2	8	3	7
Crown Royal	1.75 L	4	10	5	9
Grey Goose	1.75 L	2	12	4	10
Maker's Mark	750 ML	6	15	8	13
Black Label	1.75 L	4	16	3	17
Smirnoff Red	1.75 L	10	22	6	26
Beefeater	1.75 L	3	10	1	12
Jose Cuervo G	1.75 L	5	19	4	20

When entering your products into the spreadsheet, enter them in the order you have them set out in your bar. This way you don't have to rearrange them alphabetically each time you do inventory, and can instead just count them in their place.

Once you have your spreadsheet set up, determine what inventory periods you're going to use (weekly, monthly, etc.), and *maintain this consistency.*

When it's time to count, choose a method and stick with it. For example, if you decide to start in the front of the bar, then work your way to the back, do this every time you count. As you count, enter the data into your spreadsheet.

For bottles that aren't completely full, use decimals to represent the amount of alcohol left in the bottle. For example, if you measure the bottles in tenths, a bottle half full will be 0.5, while a bottle only 10% full will be 0.1. Enter these decimal amounts into your spreadsheet in the appropriate columns and rows.

Finally, add up the totals for each category on your spreadsheet.

At the end of your chosen period – whether it's a week, two weeks, or a month – repeat this process to get your ending inventory counts, then apply the above formula.

Here's an example calculation:

Inventory Usage = 10 bottles + 5 bottles – 3 bottles

Inventory Usage = 12 bottles

Expressed in dollars, if the average bottle of liquor costs the bar $15, the inventory usage in dollars is (12 x $15) = $180.

You can use this amount to determine how you should price your drinks based on what you want your profit margin to be.

If the average bottle serves ten drinks, then at eight bottles of inventory usage, the average cost per drink is ($180/80) = $2.25. So if you want to mark your drinks up by 50%, you should price your drinks at ($2.25/0.5) = $4.50

Over the course of the period, be sure to keep track of how much product you take in. You'll need this information to complete the calculations at the end of the period.

You want to make sure you take inventory while the bar is closed so that you don't have any distractions. Being distracted in the middle of counting can result in significant amounts of wasted time if you have to keep starting again. Additionally, make sure you train your employees on how to do bar inventory. They should be keeping records of significant spillages, breakage, or comped drinks.

Once you have your inventory calculated and you can see it alongside your sales numbers thanks to your bar POS system, you can use it to calculate pour cost, make better pricing decisions, and identify which products are the best sellers and which are the most profitable.

INVENTORY AUTOMATION

Taking inventory manually can be tedious – entering numbers into a spreadsheet takes time away from other things if you do it yourself. If you hand it off to an employee, make sure it's someone you trust and is well trained in the process.

You can work towards automating the process with a bar inventory software or inventory spreadsheet integrated into your bar point of sale system. This system can help you count, manage, and value your inventory in an all-in-one platform that can connect with your accounting, order and track inventory accurately, and set your price points wisely.

Here is a link to a POS system that can help you automate some of your inventory control stress.

https://pos.toasttab.com/restaurant-pos

The success of your bar/nightclub depends on your tracking inventory, purchases, and sales figures. Use the data you get from managing inventory to control costs, guide purchases and maintain the profit of your bar/nightclub. Consider the following steps to help you manage your alcohol inventory.

The first thing you need to do is create a spreadsheet for your current inventory. Separate liquor by categories as well as wine and beer. List everything by product name and container size. Record the cost per ounce and the cost per bottle for bottled alcohol. You should include everything in storage areas as well as the stock at the bar. Determine a specific time to do your inventory tracking, whether it is bi-weekly or monthly.

Make sure your staff and bartenders know how to account for inventory. Record items when they are moved from storage to the bar and keep track of any large spills or broken bottles. Record these transfers in a log book or separate spreadsheet. Managers can review these logs for ordering and inventory control.

At the end of each tracking period, you want to collect sales and inventory data. Track your total sales of alcohol.

You can automate your tracking by setting your cash registers to tally liquor sales for a specific period. Take an ending physical inventory and calculate the value. Compare the value of the beginning and ending inventory. The difference is considered your inventory adjustment amount.

Lastly, calculate the cost of your beverage sales. Take the cost of new stock purchased and add or subtract the inventory adjustment value so you can get the cost of beverage sales. Your beverage cost is determined by dividing your total cost of sales by your total bar sales for your designated tracking period. The resulting cost figure is the percentage of retail price that each drink costs you.

HOW TO DO AN INVENTORY

For a liquor store, inventory is a simple matter of making sure the remaining stock matches the invoice and sales records. However, the liquor inventory for a bar/nightclub is more difficult since the liquor is sold by the shot and not the bottle. It is important to take frequent inventory of your stock to make sure you're not overstocking perishable items and to make sure bartenders aren't over pouring or giving drinks away for free. Let's look at how you can do a proper inventory.

INVOICE

The first step in maintaining an inventory is to have a good organization of liquor invoices. If you don't know what's coming in then, it will be impossible to know what has been sold, spilled or given away for free. It will also make it difficult to know how much of a specific liquor needs to be stocked. The order inventory should always be done by an owner or manager, so the invoices are always organized. Check the invoice sheet with the actual bottles that are delivered each time you restock.

SALES FIGURES

Make sure you keep accurate records of how much liquor you sell each day. By doing this, you will be able to check the remaining amount of alcohol on hand against the amount of alcohol sold during an inventory period, allowing you to accurately replenish stock while also protecting against theft. There are several types of point-of-sale software that can help you track drink sales.

CONDUCTING THE ACTUAL INVENTORY

Whenever you perform an inventory, you should break your alcohols down into three main categories: beer, wine, and liquor. Liquors should also be divided into main types. Tally the number of bottles of each specific brand on hand and check the figures with your invoice sheets and sales records.

A weekly or biweekly inventory is enough as long as you don't suspect theft. If you suspect theft is occurring, then you may need to do an inventory more often until you resolve the situation. Remember you will always lose a small amount of alcohol to spillage. Make sure employees know to report significant spillage or whole bottle breaks.

PRICING, PROFITABILITY & POS

COMPETITIVE ANALYSIS

This is key to having a successful business. When you have a competitive analysis, you know your business's current position within the retail bar industry.

The competitive analysis allows you to get the information you need on your competitors, market share, market strategies, growth and other important factors. When you have all this information, you will be able to change or improve your business in key areas so you can increase profits and sales.

Here is a simple way you can do a competitive analysis. On a piece of paper write down the following:

1. Number of local competitors you have
2. What is their niche/what type of bar items they sell
3. Where they sell
4. What is their pricing

Once you have that list, take a look and see where you would fit in that list, how can you stand out from the crowd, what can you do differently that would make customers pay attention to your products.

In my business experience, I believe there are three ways you can always stand above the crowd. I always have tried to stand above the crowd by these three strategies.

1. By making superior products than my competitors make
2. By offering 100% customer satisfaction guarantee
3. By creative pricing strategy

Let me explain what I mean by creative pricing strategy.

BEST PRICING STRATEGY

Pricing is the most important factor in your business. A carefully thought out pricing strategy can make you very successful but a pricing strategy that places you above your market can literality put you out of business and on the other hand pricing below the market can wipe your bottom line profit completely clean, and before you know it, you are out of business and in debt.

That was the risky part; now the tricky part is if you stay with the market, then you are not standing *out* in the crowd, instead you are standing *in* the crowd.

In order to make yourself more visible and unique and to stand tall among other competitors, you have to be very creative when it comes to your pricing strategy, and that is where the tricky part comes in.

My goal is to teach you how to implement a carefully thought out pricing strategy that can make you stand out and make you successful.

First, we want to discuss your buying price or the price you pay you to buy your inventory, because if you don't buy at the lowest possible price then you won't be able to sell them at a competitive price, nor you will be able to keep your margin. So it is very vital that you negotiate hard and get the lowest possible price.

Now that you are buying your merchandise at a lowest possible price let's talk about the other half of this equation, the selling price and how much you should sell them for. When it comes to selling prices, this is where you have to be again very creative. Again check your local area competitors and then decide where you need to be.

Remember the best pricing strategy is where you get to keep enough margin that makes your business profitable but at the same time you are not pricing yourself out of the market.

Bar business by far has one of the best margins compared to any other QSR (quick service restaurant). It is over 70%-80% of gross profit which is huge by any standard.

Now let's discuss how we can calculate profit margin, markup and penny profit, so we all are on the same page.

Understanding Penny Profit, Profit Margin, and Markup

In business these are the three most common terms we hear every day, but what do they all mean and how they are different from each other?

Okay let's break them down and see what they are:

Penny Profit

Penny profit is essentially the actual cash profit you make by selling any items in your store. For example, say you just sold a bottle of 20 oz. Coke $1.75, what is the penny profit from that sale? To find the answer first, we need to see how much you paid to buy that bottle of Coke.

Looking at your invoice from Coke shows you paid $1.00 for that bottle of coke and you sold it for $1.75. So your penny profit is $1.75-1.00 = 75 cents. Penny profit is the difference between the selling price- actual costs.

PROFIT MARGIN

Profit margin, the term most widely used and understood in most every business, is what we all use to figure out if we are making enough profit from our businesses by selling the products and services.

Profit margin is essentially the percentage of profit you make or earn when you sell a product. Confusing? Let's take a look at the same example of that bottle of coke we just used earlier.

We already know the penny profit from that sale was 75 cents. Now the profit margin is done little differently, to find out the exact margin we will have to take the penny profit and divide that number by the selling price. So it will be $1.75-$1.00=0.75, then we divide that penny profit by the selling price 0.75/$1.75 = 43% profit margin.

MARKUP

The markup, on the other hand, is somewhat similar to profit margin, but instead of dividing the penny profit by the selling price you would have to divide the penny profit by the actual cost. Let's take a look at the same example once again.

Remember our penny profit from that bottle of Coke? It was 75 cents; now we just need to divide that by the actual cost which was a $1.00 right? Let's do this, 0.75/$1.00 = 75% Markup for that same bottle of Coke.

RIGHT PRICING

The difference between a bar's success and failure is made by setting the right price. It is fairly simple to set the right price for drinks, but you'll have to do a little math. While you buy the bottle or the crate, you are only going to be selling by the drink.

Bartenders on average pour hundreds of drinks a night, ranging from mixed drinks to cocktails. Each drink has a different ratio of different types of alcohol. To make a profit and stay competitive you need to consider the pour cost, the ratio between the price you pay and the price you sell.

Pour Cost

As I just discussed in the last chapter, your pour cost or usage cost is one very important factor to know by heart. I will try to explain the process one more time here, so everything is clear.

To determine the total pour cost for the bar, you need to take the money you spend on alcohol and divide it by the price you sell it for. For example, if your employees pour $5,000 worth of alcohol and you sell them for $25,000; then you have a pour cost of 20 percent. The higher your pour cost, the lower the percentage of profit you make from drink sales. You can also calculate individual pour costs for specific drink categories.

You can set drink prices based on a target pour cost. For example, you spend $64 for a 16-ounce bottle of alcohol, and you serve the liquor by the ounce, then you have 16 drinks in a bottle. When you divide $64 by 16, you get a $4 cost per 1 ounce drink. For a pour cost of 25 percent, $4 needs to be 25 percent of the sale price. $4 divided by 0.25 means you need to sell each drink for $16.

You may need to adjust this formula for factors such as spills, broken bottles, drink specials and strong pours. You may also need to vary your pour costs across different drinks. For example, liquors often have a higher markup than beer or wine.

However, you also want to base your pour cost on the competition as well. For example, if a 20 percent pour cost gives you 80 percent profit, but your competition is at 30 percent then you can lower your price a bit. Always keep an eye on the market and make sure you're not pricing yourself too high or too low.

Although this doesn't mean you need to check out prices at every bar/nightclub in town. Rather simply focus on your niche. Choose bars with similar themes and niches to your own and then compare your prices. You'll need to find that perfect balance between losing to your competitors and not being able to pay your employees.

Once you've been in business awhile, you should review your sales revenue and your pour cost. Consider how much you sell of each alcohol and calculate your average pour cost per category. This will allow you to determine the pour cost for total alcohol sales. If your average pour cost is too low to meet financial goals, then you'll need to increase drink prices.

Setting the right drink prices is a matter of good business judgment. Some owners choose to price on industry standards or 18 to 24 percent pour cost, while others go for a lower pour cost to stay competitive. You can also look into improving pour costs by reducing spending. For example, if you reduce spillage, you will increase profits without having to raise your prices.

PROPER GROSS PROFIT FOR A BAR INVENTORY

A bar/nightclub drink inventory needs to have a high-profit margin of no less than the low 80 percent range since it is needed to cover other expenses. To stay in this area, you need to think about pour cost, which is the inverse of the gross profit margin. As we discussed before the pour cost can vary based on several variables. First, let's look at why 80 percent is the right number.

WHY 80 PERCENT?

While 80 percent may seem like a high-profit margin, stocking the bar/nightclub drink inventory likely only represents a small portion of the actual operating costs for the bar. Statistics show that the cost of alcohol is often only about 40 percent of the monthly costs for operating a bar/nightclub. Also, while you might price your inventory to generate a profit margin of 80 to 85 percent, liquor losses also tend to run high. Your 80 percent gross profit margin is likely to drop to 75 percent when you add in a 25 percent liquor loss factor.

GROSS PROFITS BY ALCOHOL TYPE

Each type of alcohol in your inventory should have a different profit margin. For example, liquor should have a profit margin of 80 to 85 percent while beer should have a margin of about 80 percent. Bottled beer can have a margin of about 75 percent and wine can even be 60 to 70 percent. More expensive drinks also tend to have a lower margin than cheaper drinks.

MARGINS AND PROFITS

Bottled wine is an excellent example of where a gross profit margin can be misleading. For example, a cheap bottle of wine can be marked up three and a half times to make an $8 bottle cost $28 a bottle with a 71.4 percent gross margin. On the other hand, an expensive bottle of wine may be marked up by double to make a $30 bottle cost $60 a bottle with a 50 percent gross margin. While the second bottle of wine has a lower margin, the actual profit is higher than the first bottle.

MANAGING PROFITS

Getting the most profit from your drink inventory is a two-step process. You first want to control losses by making sure the highest possible proportion of the alcohol you purchase goes into drinks. The second step is to not focus too strongly on your profit margin. While a higher margin is better, if you can sell high-end cocktails at a higher profit per drink then a lower profit margin isn't as significant.

POS SYSTEM

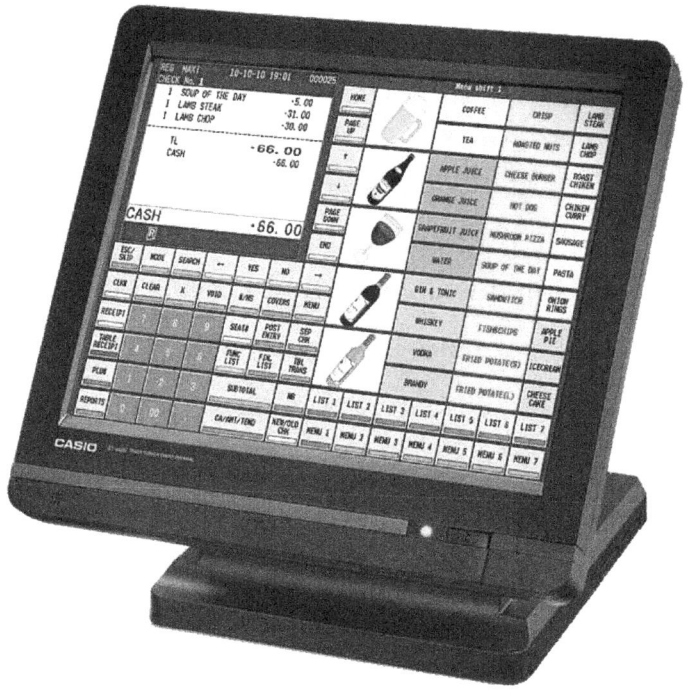

Without an efficient and reliable point of sale system, your business can be slowed down by lags in payment processing, poor inventory management and untimely services and repairs. But if your POS is cloud-based, you won't have to worry about tracking your data or inventory because the system will help you do it all. Luckily, cloud-based POS systems are not only lightning fast, but reliable as well.

But these systems are so much more than bundles of software and hardware. In one ergonomic terminal, you will also have the power to track your business' analytics and profits, keep track of inventory, and oversee email marketing to bring in new customers.

You may not need all items on this bar equipment list. There is no absolute recipe for success when opening a bar. To understand what will work for you, be aware of the demographic you are serving as well as their needs and wants. Do not buy equipment that you do not need or are unsure about how to use.

When buying new equipment always be aware of the wide-eye syndrome. Let's face it some things just look cool, and we want them, but this is not the place for impulse buying. That money would be better spent on things you need. Buying things that appear fancy and high-tech will lead you nowhere.

There are dozens of efficient Point of Sale systems out there, and all of them offer great functions to effectively run your bar. As the use of tablets and Wi-Fi have changed the process of ringing up customers and tracking products, there have been many updates to keep up with the change of pace. The following are three of the most functional POS software to get you started with the basics of what you should look for in a system!

As I just mentioned, here is a great bar POS system you can look at and try a demo.

https://pos.toasttab.com/restaurant-pos

ACCOUNTING & BOOKKEEPING

ACCOUNTING BASICS AND TIPS

As a business owner, it's difficult to hand the financial reigns over to someone else. You may feel like they are not as passionate about your business as you are and may not trust them to handle your finances the way you normally would.

But, it's important to hire an accountant to take care of your bar's accounting needs. Running any type of restaurant can be overwhelming, and managing the books is one way to outsource the task, so you have free time to focus on other departments of your business.

Staying organized and keeping track of the numbers are only two effective strategies to keep your profits in-line with your long-term fiscal goals. Keep reading to learn the basics of finding a good accountant and tips for practicing the best accounting methods.

1. Shop Around First

Network with other restaurant and bar owners to find out how they manage their accounting records. Making acquaintances with industry professionals will give you great insight on how to handle your books and correctly keep records.

2. Strive for Accuracy

Although this is common sense to most, keeping precise records of your bar's finances is crucial to success. Do not ever round your numbers or use estimations. Exact amounts of money for all revenue is one of the key factors in whether or not a business excels. Compromising on a few cents will start to add up over time.

3. Ask for Monthly P&L

P&L stands for profit and loss. A profit and loss statement is one method of tracking a restaurant's revenue, labor and food costs, and operating expenses. A P&L statement stores all of your bar's accounting information into one cohesive document that can then be customized to fit your independent needs. Along with creating a P&L, you will also need to make a detailed breakdown of the bar's costs and revenue to better understand the P&L. (Refer back to the P&L I shared earlier in this book)

4. Invest in Restaurant Accounting Software

Financial software and POS systems are helpful tools when organizing inventory and transactions swiftly and precisely. Depending on what accounting software you are using, you can also handle payroll, alternate methods of payment, and sales records.

MUSIC AND ROYALTIES

Music for your establishment seems like a simple situation that doesn't need much focus and discussion, but you would be wrong. Think of all the bars/nightclubs you've been to, they all tend to play the same music. So why would you want to stick to the same music as all the other competition?

Again it comes down to cost. Playing music in your establishment is going to cost you in royalties. When you play any type of music in your establishment, you are going to pay royalties in the form of a license that is renewable each year.

ASCAP and BMI are the two main licensing agencies that will charge you an annual fee to play recorded or live music in your establishment.

The price you are charged will vary depending on your seating capacity or by the square foot. This is often a hidden cost of starting a bar/nightclub that many aren't aware of.

MAINTENANCE AND CLEANING

When you are getting your establishment started, one of the last things on your mind is cleaning. There are so many other concerns with regards to planning and financing that you probably haven't given much thought to cleaning or the supplies needed.

However, cleaning is an essential and important part of owning a bar/nightclub. Not only are there unannounced visits by the health inspector, but you also don't want to drive away customers or cause tension among the staff with a poorly cleaned establishment.

How you handle the cleaning will vary depending on your establishment. A smaller establishment where you are pretty much the sole employee won't require a lot of planning. However, if you have employees or you are a larger establishment, then you may want to consider hiring a cleaning crew. For most, they choose to assign the cleaning duties to the employees.

The key to an effective cleaning among employees is to have a checklist and assign specific people to specific tasks. In general, employees should be responsible for cleaning their own stations. For example, the bartenders would be responsible for cleaning the bar area at the end of the night. For common areas such as the bathroom, you should have a rotating schedule so each employee takes a turn and no one feels singled out for bathroom cleaning.

MAINTENANCE

Cleaning is only one part of making your establishment successful; you also need to maintain it properly. If you neglect little things, it can have a domino effect on your entire operation. Regular maintenance keeps everyone safe and saves you money.

Each aspect of your business needs its own maintenance schedule. Make sure these are a part of the job description for whoever you feel is responsible. If your establishment grows large enough, you may consider hiring a maintenance person to do any repair work as needed. Until then you should simply choose one day a week that you come in to deal with any maintenance issues.

Maintenance needs to include both interior and exterior. People aren't going to be lining up to enter your establishment if the outside looks rundown.

Keep the outside looking clean and tidy to encourage people to come into your establishment. Inside you should focus on items that customers see and that affect things like your alcohol storage and dispensing.

MARKETING AND PROMOTION

The type of patrons you want in your establishment will determine the type of marketing and promotional methods you use. You need to find the right mix since some individuals are looking for what's popular while others are looking for something unique they won't find anywhere else. Consider the following ideas to help you get people into your establishment.

The first thing to consider is special events. Consider a theme night or an event that targets a specific demographic group you are interested in attracting. Some options include a battle of the local bands, a karaoke night, a Mardi Gras themed party or any other number of ideas.

Consider doing a contest with prizes. Host a contest similar to those popular on TV right now with singing, dancing, and entertainment to draw people to your establishment. Offer prizes to the winners and encourage the audience to participate. You can also plan something that benefits the community such as a food drive that gets people entered into a drawing to win prizes.

Offer a VIP club for regular patrons so they will feel a part of an exclusive group. Some special benefits you can offers include free food or drinks. You can also offer unique prizes to VIP members when they introduce new patrons. Lastly, reward these loyal patrons with a member's only event once a year.

Lastly, try focused advertising that appeals to the demographics you want to attract. Send a text message to younger customers asking them to a special theme night for their age group. Use social media to have a strong online presence. Consider handing out coupons to areas frequented by your suggested patrons offering free drinks at your establishment.

ONLINE & OFFLINE MARKETING

Make your bar business the new thing that your customers are obsessed with. Also, people are most likely to trust the reviews of the people they know so a positive word of mouth review can go a long way.

While Social media is not a new marketing strategy anymore, it still is very effective one. Small business has a huge advantage with social media. Using these platforms to connect with people in your area can help your business feel like part of the community.

It is a free and easy way to publicize specials and events and show off people having a great time at your bar. You can also offer specials like private parties or a room for painting parties, or share special recipes for cocktails to connect with your customer base. Customers will respond to this positively and will tell others the really nice thing that you did for them.

Connecting with your surrounding community is essential to your success. Bar businesses rely heavily on the relationships they cultivate with their customers. Social media is a great start, but being active online is just not enough. However, there are some great ways to ingrain yourself in the community.

One method is to sponsor an event close to everyone's heart. Whether that be a festival or a charity run or anything that brings in an excited crowd. Showing your brand at these big town events help endear the people to you as well as helps you to gain additional customers.

Making sure that the community feels that you are with them, will make them want to be with you. These will be the customers that you will grow to rely on.

You can also, have in-house events such as live bands playing once a month. Having a Ladies' Night or Guys' Night can be popular. Getting customers in your shop, and having a good time is a great way to connect with future customers.

If you put on events that everyone is excited about, then you have helped to make yourself a destination for the community. If they come for an event, they just might come back with a friend the next day.

Customer reviews are importantly similar to word of mouth. People like to hear reviews from other real people, even if they do not know those people. That means the better reviews you have online, the better your business will most likely do. There are several things you can do to obtain positive reviews.

The first thing is always to have a great product line and great customer service. You cannot have positive reviews from customers who don't have positive experiences. The easiest way to get reviews on sites like Yelp is to ask your customers directly. After filling a customer's order, ask that customer to rate their experience on a website like Yelp. A simple reminder will result in more reviews from people who might not have thought to do so.

You can also place a sign near the entrance or have that be the home screen of Yelp when anyone logs in to the free Wi-Fi. Encouraging people to posit reviews. If these reminders aren't doing enough to get you a satisfactory amount of reviews, try offering a discount to anyone who provides a screenshot of the review they made.

Emphasize that even if it is a negative review, they will still receive the discount, and you will do whatever needs to be done to make their experiences better in the future.

When considering marketing, graphic design is one of the first things that should come to mind. With the help of a great graphic designer, you will be able to make a cohesive visual marketing strategy.

The first thing you have to do is find a graphic designer you work well with. In order to find the best graphic designer for you, you need to consider your wants and needs. If you're in the market for small jobs, your best bet is sites like Fiverr.com or for bigger jobs try 99designs.com.

These online talent platforms gather many graphic designers from all around the world. You can either post your job and let talents bid on them, or you can look through various profiles and read their reviews then hire someone directly.

It is best to describe your job requirements in detail. Let's assume you want a new logo. The first thing you want to do is write down all your needs, color choices and provide some logo designs you like from other companies. Don't worry, you are not trying to copy from other companies, but showing them what type of logos you want.

You also would say the scalability you want for the logo. If you want a logo for business cards, you should say so, even if that means you have to have different but very similar logos for different sizes.

Remember to make sure that your logo makes sense in grayscale, and for those that are red-green colorblind. At the end of your description, you want to detail the price that you feel is fair for your project.

You can get a logo done at Fiverr.com for $5, but it may not be what you want or suitable to your liking, the next best option is 99designs.com. This site is little more expensive but well worth it.

You can also use more general classifieds like Craigslist in your area, or freelancer websites like upwork.com, freelancer.com, and guru.com that connect you with many types of freelancers. Using many methods can create a large variety of candidates you'll have to look through. That means you will need to be rigorous with your choosing process, described next.

So after you've messaged several candidates, you now have to choose just one graphic designer, unlike other jobs, rely on portfolios instead of resumes. Make sure that you consider whether you like their prior work.

Designers will not change their style to match yours; they never deviate from their own chosen style. You cannot force them to see your vision, instead, take some time to find the kind of person whose vision matches your own. That is where you would really succeed.

The next thing you want to do is call their references. However, don't get excited when their references are positive. They wouldn't be listed as references, otherwise

Instead, you're looking for amazing recommendations. Things that go beyond saying they are good to work with. You want to hear how amazing this graphic designer is, how they wouldn't work for anyone else. Most importantly they need to rave about them always delivering on time and budget.

Once you are fully satisfied, go ahead and hire the designer of your choice.

Make sure to get things in writing, so there's no confusion when it comes time for payment.

The contract should state that you get all of the electronic source files of all works, this is important so that you can make any small changes by yourself or switch to an entirely different designer.

The very last thing that needs to be found before you're ready to put your graphic designer to work is to get to know each other. You want to figure out how to work together.

The designer will want things like a clear direction, so give them that direction. If you are unsure, bring that confusion to the table and work with your graphic designer and come up with a solution. Don't let your graphic designer muddy your vision, but also don't be so confusing to the point where no one even knows your vision.

Just take things one step at a time when it comes to the design work. Instead of making a grand plan for everything, start small. For example, just focus on choosing the best color scheme and an interesting logo first.

After you get the basics totally finished and approved. You will have a much easier time getting the rest to fall into place. Once your colors, attitude, and style are embodied in something as iconic as a logo, the path to websites, white papers, blogs, and tradeshow banners becomes an extension of an idea rather than a new project.

Finally, "baby-steps" means you can spend only what you want. If you end up not liking to work with each other or what you want ends up being too expensive, you can stop and still have something to show for it for your next designer, or maybe you can try to do the rest yourself.

PROVEN MARKETING IDEAS

Without marketing ideas and tactics you will find a reduced customer base and depleted profit margins. Implementing marketing strategies can help you have a flourishing establishment. If you aren't getting enough customers, then you need to make some changes.

The tried and true method is to offer specials and promotions. Two for one drinks, theme nights and other specials and promotions are popular marketing tools; but only if you advertise it right. The best thing is to have a social media profile. Distribute flyers to locations in your area that are frequented by the patrons you want to attract to your establishment in order to promote your specials.

Drinking customers will eventually get hungry; so it can be a good idea to offer finger foods and/or snack items to extend customers stay. You can install a kitchen to make these foods, but you will need to get the associated licenses and permits; plus you will have to weigh the cost of installing a kitchen.

Consider hosting an event to spread the recognition of your establishment. It can be a charity event or anything that promotes something close to your establishment theme so you can increase patron traffic. Hosting events is a great way to increase your profile in the community while also getting free publicity.

There are quite a few marketing tools available to bars/nightclubs, but only a few are going to be effective for your establishment. You need to pick and choose the right marketing tactics for you. Some marketing tools such as emails, newsletters, press releases, websites and social media can be used by all establishments. However, there are certain promotions and specials that need to be catered to your specific theme and style.

CREATING A BUZZ

As a bar/nightclub owner, you are not only competing with other establishments, but you are also competing for the limited time that people have for recreational purposes. This is why you need to successfully promote your establishment. The goal is to get people into your establishment and create a buzz. The following steps take you through how to successfully promote your establishment.

The first thing you need to do is develop a budget for your overall promotion. While a new establishment is going to have a smaller marketing budget, it is important that you don't cut corners. You should plan to have at least one-third of your promotional budget going to marketing. Start promoting about eight weeks in advance and use any strategies that are within your promotional budget. Your promotions need to be planned, so they increase in frequency and size until the final event.

Look for local sponsors who will cross-promote the event with you. A lot of places will allow you to promote your establishment in exchange for their own advertisement at your establishment promotion.

While we are in a digital age, don't forget to develop a print marketing strategy as well. Consider advertising in alternative publications that reach a niche audience of those you want to attract to your establishment. If you can afford it, try to run print ads for at least two months.

Hang flyers both in your club and the surrounding neighborhood weeks in advance. Locate areas that are in the same niche as your establishment to attract the right patrons.

Lastly, in today's digital world don't neglect online marketing tools like Facebook. If your budget allows you can also use a stand-alone website for promotion as well.

HOW TO INCREASE LIQUOR SALES

All bars/nightclubs sell the same alcohol. You need to work to get people to come to your establishment, and then you need to exceed their expectations, so they stay longer. The way to make them stay longer is to have new and interesting cocktails. Use the following tips to help you increase liquor sales at your establishment.

The first thing you need to do is prepare. Make sure your back bar is organized and that you have no deadstock. Make sure premium products are easily accessible and that you have enough inventory on hand to handle an increase in demand.

Next, you need to come up with a signature cocktail for your establishment. This is easier than you may be thinking. The goal is to make it both delicious and visually attractive. Perhaps use a glass that is different from all other drinks. Having a unique cocktail can be the greatest achievement of your establishment.

In addition to a unique cocktail, you should also consider adding a unique infusion to the list. Nearly any liquor can be turned into a unique drink by infusing it with something unique like cinnamon. Place the liquor in a large container and marinate with fruit or spice for five to seven days. This can give you something unique to offer from all the other establishments.

Lastly, consider making up some alcohol-free cocktails for those who don't want to drink, but still want to hang out with their friends. Make the drink appealing so people will want to stay and mingle with other patrons.

Come up with new and unique ideas by having monthly contests among your staff to come up with recipes. Also, consider competitions among staff to get them to offer and sell more of the unique cocktails to customers.

Once you have a unique drink menu, you need an in-house marketing plan to sell them. The menu needs to complement your decor and theme. Have the new cocktails displayed on every table with a description that emphasizes their qualities. Also, train your staff to offer the new cocktails as suggestions to customers.

HOW TO UPSELL LIQUOR

Bartenders and servers are presented with several options for upselling drinks, but it can be difficult to convince the patron. The key when it comes to upselling liquor is to make sure your staff knows the products and use a helpful and consultative approach. There are several ways you can do this.

The first part is to make sure your staff becomes experts. Upselling becomes successful when customers view your staff as liquor experts who can offer sound advice. You want staff that are knowledgeable about in-stock liquors as well as out-of-stock items that may become available. The staff needs to know types, brands, and locations of all alcohol stocked in your bar/nightclub. Bartenders need to know the difference between rail, call, and top-shelf liquor; as well as the brands within each category. Each brand has their own origins and tastes that need to be understood. Lastly, it is important that everyone knows the buying trends of customers. Know when top-selling liquors sell on which days.

Once your staff has the necessary knowledge, it is important to work on the actual sales tactics. Rather than using hard tactics, it is important to train your staff to use anticipation and trust. Don't repeatedly ask customers if they want a drink or constantly bring up discounts and specials. Rather, build trust in your patrons by anticipating their best choices to increase impulse buying and repeat orders.

Make sure all staff members know the names of repeat customers along with their favorite drinks. Then make sure the liquors needed for these drinks are always in stock. Based on the drinking habits of repeat customers you should also stock similar liquors they might like. Repeat customers will appreciate this effort and may be more likely to try new or more expensive alcohol because they will know the staff is trying to help them have a more enjoyable experience.

Another sales tactic to train your staff in is to upsell drinks by suggesting certain brands over others, such as offering premium brands or those you are trying to sell. This can also help when educating customers on specific brands tastes when either drank alone or mixed with other alcohols and foods.

ADDITIONAL REVENUE IDEAS

A bar/nightclub has a lot of competition; not only from other drinking establishments but also from restaurants and even liquor stores. Getting people into your establishment isn't the only issue, but you also need to make sure they continue to spend money once inside. This means using a variety of revenue ideas to keep your establishment new, interesting and fun.

Consider starting or joining a crawl event to get new people into your establishment and split revenues with other establishments. Bar or pub crawls are typically done when establishments are within walking distance of each other and can be heavily advertised in the local area.

You can also branch out into non-drink related sales. If you have a unique logo that people are interested in, then consider offering items for sale with your logo. The items should be bar related such as pint glasses, coasters, t-shirts, etc. Often these items are cheaper when purchased in bulk so you can have a decent profit margin.

If you have a specific day or time that your establishment isn't that busy, then consider finding other ways to use your facility. Perhaps you can rent it out for special events or gatherings. You'll need to talk to a zoning official or a lawyer to make sure you have the required permits and meet the appropriate regulations.

KEEPING THINGS FRESH AND NEW

At some point, you may need to reinvent your establishment out of necessity. Whether you opened the wrong type of establishment in the wrong area or things simply start to change around you; there is going to be a time when you need to reinvent yourself to stay successful.

If you find your revenues shrinking and your best marketing efforts aren't helping, then it may be time to think about reinventing your establishment rather than keep pouring money into marketing efforts. Reinventing your establishment will be like opening a new place all over again, and you'll be able to attract a new group of patrons.

Most of your major costs are already invested in the business so you'll only need to do a minor cosmetic change to be ready to go. Just remember to make sure you leave nothing familiar behind and completely reinvent yourself.

Last but not least, here a couple of links to Professional Bartending Guides (Downloadable pdf files) that you can click and download and customize for your own company then hand them over to your new employees. There are hundreds of recipes that you can test and try.

http://www.wordsyouwant.com/professionalbartender.pdf

http://swizzle.ru/uploads/article_file/17/mr_boston.pdf

http://www.restaurantfiles.talktalk.net/Basic_Knowledge/Customer%20service%20manual.pdf

LAST WORD

I want to say THANK YOU for purchasing and reading this book. I really hope you got a lot out of it!

Can I ask you for a quick favor though?

If you enjoyed this book, I would really appreciate it if you could leave me a Review.

I LOVE getting feedback from my wonderful readers, and reviews do make the difference. I read all of my reviews and would love to hear your thoughts.

Thank you so much!!

Made in the
USA
Monee, IL